At Issue

Is the American Dream
a Myth?

Other books in the At Issue series:

At Issue

Is the American Dream a Myth?

Kate Burns, Book Editor

GREENHAVEN PRESS

An imprint of Thomson Gale, a part of The Thomson Corporation

THOMSON

GALE

Detroit • New York • San Francisco • New Haven, Conn. • Waterville, Maine • London • Munich

Bonnie Szumski, *Publisher*
Helen Cothran, *Managing Editor*

© 2006 Thomson Gale, a part of The Thomson Corporation.

Thomson and Star logo are trademarks and Gale and Greenhaven Press are registered trademarks used herein under license.

For more information, contact:
Greenhaven Press
27500 Drake Rd.
Farmington Hills, MI 48331-3535
Or you can visit our Internet site at http://www.gale.com

LIBRARY OF CONGRESS CATALOGING-IN-PUBLICATION DATA

Is the American dream a myth? / Kate Burns, book editor.
    p. cm. – (At issue)
Includes bibliographical references and index.
ISBN 0-7377-3493-0 (hardcover lib. : alk. paper) -- ISBN 0-7377-3494-9
(pbk. : alk. paper)
    1. American Dream. 2. United States--Social conditions--21st century. 3. United States–Economic conditions--21st century. 4. Social mobility--United States.
5. Quality of life–United States. I. Burns, Kate, 1963– II. Series: At issue
(San Diego, Calif.)
    HN59.2. I79 2007
    306.0973'090511–dc22
                                                      2006016635

Printed in the United States of America
10 9 8 7 6 5 4 3 2 1

Contents

Introduction

The theme of the American dream has inspired many artists, writers, politicians, and teachers for decades. Every year, students and professional writers, both native-born and immigrants, write many essays exploring their beliefs about the American dream. Politicians invoke the dream in speeches, teachers develop class plans to study the dream, and Hollywood returns to the dream in movie after movie, to the delight of millions of filmgoers. Many people nod with understanding when the dream is mentioned because it has become a powerful symbol of the aspirations of a nation of immigrants. Yet the phrase "the American dream" is misleading because it implies that there is only *one* dream. In fact, there are many versions of the American dream, and how people define it depends greatly on their age, cultural identity, and citizenship status.

In 2004 the National League of Cities (NLC) conducted a survey of more than one thousand participants aged eighteen and older, asking them what they considered the American dream to be. The NLC found that for the majority of Americans—adults aged twenty-three to sixty-five—material prosperity is at the heart of the American dream. For many this prosperity is symbolized by home ownership. The hope that children will be able to build on the success of their parents and rise to a higher social class is also a central aspect of the American dream for millions of Americans and immigrants. As the Aspen Institute, a research institute on American culture and policy, proclaims, "the opportunity to save, invest [in the future] and own is the foundation of the American dream."

For many adults older than sixty-five, however, financial abundance takes second place to quality of life in their vision of the American dream. Over one-fourth of the older respondents of the NLC survey rated the ability to enjoy good health as the primary priority, in contrast to only 5 percent of the eighteen- to twenty-nine-year-old respondents. Author Gary Goshgarian also describes the importance of health in his best-selling popular culture anthology *The Contemporary Reader*:

> Healthiness is a part of the American Dream that everyone seems to overlook. I believe that when it comes to living a so called 'perfect life' there is nothing more important than having good health. A person can have all the money in the world; a person can have all the spare time in the world; a person can have the most loving family in the world; however, what good is all of this if he or she is dying from an incurable disease?

Young Americans aged eighteen to twenty-nine also hold a view of the American dream in which prosperity is secondary. According to the NLC survey, over 45 percent of the younger respondents believe that living in freedom is the most important aspect of the American dream. Twenty-five-year-old Chris Hueter explains this version of the dream on his "Magnifisyncopathological" Web site. "The bedrock underneath [the dream]," writes Hueter, "is the fundamental right to one's life and to decide how to live it. When people dream about saving lives through medicine, becoming President, making themselves rich, or quietly living with those [they] love, what they are really dreaming about is the freedom to do so."

For many Americans the American dream is living in a country where all citizens have equal rights and opportunities. For example, American minorities who have experienced discrimination tend to envision a dream that eliminates inequality and prejudice. In a famous speech made on the steps of the Lincoln Memorial in Washington, D.C., on August 28, 1963, Martin Luther King Jr. described the essence of this dream. Before thousands of onlookers, he said:

I have a dream that one day this nation will rise up and live out the true meaning of its creed: "We hold these truths to be self-evident, that all men are created equal."

I have a dream that one day on the red hills of Georgia, the sons of former slaves and the sons of former slave owners will be able to sit down together at the table of brotherhood.

I have a dream that one day even the state of Mississippi, a state sweltering with the heat of injustice, sweltering with the heat of oppression, will be transformed into an oasis of freedom and justice.

King's American dream that all citizens will someday receive equal protection under the U.S. Constitution and will live in a nation where "they will not be judged by the color of their skin but by the content of their character" is a dream held by many in America.

The dream of equality encompasses the dream of having the right to own land—a right that for many years was denied to African Americans—women, and other minorities. Author Audrey Edwards describes the history of injustices African Americans have faced:

For more than 300 years we were slaves in America, which by definition excluded us from owning anything at all. And even when we were freed and told we might receive 40 acres and a mule following the Civil War, it was a proposal soon undermined. Indeed, much of our history with land and property ownership in America has revolved around our seeing it stolen, burned to the ground, redlined or denied through blockbusting.

Although discrimination still exists, since the civil rights movement more African Americans have achieved the dream of owning a home and having financial security.

For many immigrants the American dream is about enjoying civil rights as well as the opportunity to gain economic security. This is especially true for new Americans emigrating from countries that suppress political and religious diversity and persecute those who disagree with the government. Tehreem Rehman, a Pakistani student from New York, writes, "My dad came here because he wanted more opportunities, better living standards, equal rights, and most of all his freedom. He wanted freedom of speech, thought, and worship." Immigrants who have been oppressed in other nations take solace in the words inscribed on the pedestal of the Statue of Liberty:

> Give me your tired, your poor,
> Your huddled masses yearning to
> be free,
> The wretched refuse of your teem-
> ing shore.
> Send these, the homeless, tempest-
> tost to me,
> I lift my lamp beside the golden
> door!

In the twenty-first century millions of Americans continue to pursue the American dream, however they envision it. In *At Issue: Is the American Dream a Myth?* Americans from many backgrounds debate whether these dreams of economic opportunity, personal liberty, and civil rights are still within reach in America. Given the importance of these dreams to society, having a greater understanding of these debates is crucial.

1

The American Dream Still Exists

Matthew Warshauer

Matthew Warshauer is a professor of American history at Central Connecticut State University and is currently writing two books about President Andrew Jackson.

The American dream has always included achieving financial success; however, the celebrated method of acquiring money has changed over the centuries of American history. Early versions of the American dream honored thrift and hard work as the preferred way to become successful. Since the industrial revolution, however, Americans have dreamed about finding shortcuts to extravagant wealth, including winning on lucrative game shows or buying a lucky lottery ticket. Some people have also attempted to win millions of dollars in lawsuits in their pursuit of the American dream of instant wealth. The emphasis on good fortune rather than industriousness and perseverance is eroding the work ethic that once made the American dream a respectable goal.

Traditionally, Americans have sought to realize the American dream of success, fame and wealth through thrift and hard work. However, the industrialization of the 19th and 20th centuries began to erode the dream, replacing it with a philosophy of "get rich quick". A variety of seductive but elusive strategies have evolved, and today the three leading ways to instant wealth are large-prize television game shows, big-jackpot state lotteries and compensation lawsuits.

Matthew Warshauer, "Who Wants to Be a Millionaire: Changing Conceptions of the American Dream," *American Studies Today Online*, February 2003. Reproduced by permission of the publisher and the author.

How does one achieve the American Dream? The answer undoubtedly depends upon one's definition of the Dream, and there are many from which to choose. John Winthrop envisioned a religious paradise in a "City upon a Hill." Martin Luther King, Jr. dreamed of racial equality. Both men yearned for what they perceived as perfection. Scholars have recognized widely varying conceptions of these quests for American excellence. One component of the American Dream seems, however, to be fairly consistent: the quest for money. Few will deny that Americans are intently focused on the "almighty dollar." In a society dedicated to capitalism and the maxim that, "the one who dies with the most toys wins," the ability to purchase a big house and a nice car separates those who are considered successful from those who are not. Yet the question remains, how does one achieve this success? How is the Dream realized? For many Americans the formula is one of instant, albeit elusive, gratification. Rather than adhering to a traditional work ethic, far too many Americans are pinning their hopes on what they perceive as "easy" money. This article focuses on three phenomena in contemporary American society that have successfully captured the quest for the American Dream. Savvy marketers have convinced their audiences that a new wave of television game shows, lottery luck, and lucrative lawsuits are the way to wealth.

Rags to Riches Through Thrift and Hard Work

Instant wealth has not always been a major component of the Dream. Americans have traditionally centered their efforts on thrift and hard work. During the Colonial Period, Benjamin Franklin counseled people on the "The Way to Wealth." *Poor Richard's Almanac* advised that "Early to Bed, and early to rise, makes a Man healthy, wealthy, and wise." The key to wealth was industry: "Industry pays debts," insisted Poor Richard. Americans of the Early Republic expanded Franklin's notion of industry into a labor ideology. For many the goal was not extravagant wealth, but, rather, economic independence and the opportunity for social advancement through financial gain. Abraham Lincoln insisted that the greatness of the American North was that industry allowed all men to prosper: "The prudent, penniless beginner in the world, labors for wages awhile, saves a surplus with which to buy tools or land, for himself; then labors on his own account another while, and at length hires another new beginner to help him. This . . . is free labor—the just and generous, and prosperous system, which opens the way for all."

Many Americans no longer entertain a vision for the future that includes time, sweat, and ultimate success.

In the midst of industrialization following the Civil War, many Americans experienced profound hardship in the changing economic landscape. They found solace in the tales of Horatio Alger, whose characters overcame adversity through industry, perseverance, self-reliance, and self-discipline. The ubiquitous "rags to riches" legend became a cornerstone of American society; anyone could succeed and achieve wealth if they worked hard. The commitment to industry illustrated by Alger's characters, Lincoln's ideals of free labor, and Franklin's practical maxims were further solidified in the American mind by the addition of a religiously based, Protestant "work ethic." Many believed that hard work allowed one to not only achieve financial success, but, through that success, revealed God's grace.

Numerous scholars note that the shift away from the traditional American work ethic corresponded directly with the rise of industry. Work values changed dramatically when the assembly line production and machine driven atmosphere of industrial America swallowed up skilled workers. The aftermath of World War II exacerbated the ethical shift as a consumer culture blossomed and Americans became preoccupied with material goods. As one critic [David Reisman] noted, "consumed by desires for status, material goods, and acceptance, Americans apparently had lost the sense of individuality, thrift, hard work, and craftsmanship that had characterized the nation."

The result of this shift in work ethic has actually spurred rather than lessened the people's desire to achieve the American Dream. Yet the real difference is that the Dream has become more of an entitlement than something to work towards. Many Americans no longer entertain a vision for the future that includes time, sweat, and ultimate success. Rather, they covet the shortcut to wealth. Many who are engaged in work view it more as a necessary evil until striking it rich. This idea has been perpetuated by a massive marketing effort that legitimizes the message that wealth can be obtained quickly and easily. Whether through the television entertainment industry, state-based lottery marketing drives, or legal advertisements, Americans are told again and again that the road to the financial success of the American Dream is more a matter of luck than hard work.

"Who Wants to Be a Millionaire"

Little reveals the shift in the quest for the American Dream more than the insanely popular television game show, "Who Wants to Be a Millionaire," hosted by Regis Philbin. With an average two hundred and forty thousand people per calling in on "Contest Day" attempting to become contestants, and a twenty-nine million per show viewing audience, it is safe to say that Americans are captivated by what many consider to be an easy avenue to achieving financial success. The fact that "Millionaire" was originally a British television show merely emphasizes the extent to which the quest for cash transcends national borders. It is no surprise, however, that the show achieved its greatest success in America. The very title of the show capitalizes on the core of the American Dream: wads of cash. The question, "Who Wants to Be a Millionaire?" is a no-brainer. The American desire to be rich is at the very heart of our nation's capitalist economy. The show's producers have simply tapped into a value already prevalent in today's society. In doing so, the show has become both a reflection of and a catalyst to greed and materialism.

What sets apart "Who Wants to Be a Millionaire" from game shows of the past is the sheer amount that a contestant can win, combined with what at times seem to be amazingly easy questions. Five players achieved the $1,000,000 mark in 2000, and two more won the top prize in 2001. Dozens have won upwards of $500,000. In addition to the high rewards, "Who Wants to Be a Millionaire" is successful because the average viewers see themselves as potential winners. One does not need to be a "Jeopardy" brainiac to answer what word was spelled backwards on the mirror in the movie "The Shining." It was "murder" of course. Or, even more simple, what do the rings on the inner part of a tree signify?

The large jackpots and relative ease of "Who Wants to Be a Millionaire" is what places it in the realm of the American Dream. Game shows of the past generally provided new appliances, trips, or cash winnings in the tens of thousands. This new breed of big money game show fits the Dream because it capitalizes both on the psychology and spectacle of being a "millionaire," as well as the idea that anyone can achieve this success. The latter fits directly into the tradition that all individuals who are willing to work hard can achieve financial reward. . . .

"Who Wants to Be a Millionaire"'s success is directly related to the belief that anyone with a little knowledge and a lot of luck can be a millionaire. Such a message resonates with the mass of people specifically because it seems to make the American Dream so easily accessible. In the process, the most basic, traditional means of achieving the Dream, industry, has been eradicated. Poor Richard's counsel to engage in "industry" is unnecessary in such a schema. Nowhere in Franklin's writings did it say, "early to bed, early to rise, hope for some luck and you might win a prize." . . .

State Lotteries

"Who Wants to Be a Millionaire" and similar game shows are only the latest craze in capitalizing on the American Dream. Even more well known, and often more lucrative are state-run lotteries. All one needs is "A Buck and a Dream," boasts the New York Lottery. Just as in the game shows, the lottery focuses on the hope of easy money with minimal effort. One does not need to work hard in order to choose a series of numbers. In the lottery scenario, one works for a living only until they hit that big Lotto or Powerball score. The Illinois Lottery's advertisement in a Chicago ghetto encouraged, "This could be your ticket out."

Whereas the payoffs for the big jackpot lotteries are significantly higher than the "Millionaire" games, a May 2000 Powerball game reached 350 million, the odds of winning are equally long. With an average 1 in 12 to 14 million chance of winning, and 1 in 80 million for the big prizes, the degree of luck needed is astronomical. Still, Americans flock to the lottery when the possibility of scoring big is most remote. In 1998, a 300 million dollar jackpot caused thousands of New Yorkers to flood across Connecticut state lines. Greenwich, Connecticut stores had lines 500 people long waiting upwards of 6 hours to purchase tickets. Forced to deal with traffic gridlock and disorderly conduct, the town was forced to spend some $80,000 for police and other emergency services. During the same Powerball drawing, the New Hampshire Lottery executive director held a press conference requesting people not to spend beyond their limits. Notwithstanding such warnings, one man admitted dishing out $3,000 for tickets.

The Powerball and Lotto frenzy is easy to explain: most everyone believes in the American Dream. And though the majority will admit that winning is a long shot, they nevertheless fantasize about the possibility. Having that kernel of hope is part of the Dream. It is the state lotteries' ability to capitalize on this fantasy that makes them so successful. Operating in 37 states and the District of Columbia, lotteries sales for 1996 totaled 42.9 billion dollars, 38% of which was net revenue, making lotteries by far the most profitable form of gambling. Most gambling venues pay back about 90% of what they take in, whereas lotteries pay out only about 50%.

> *Americans are sent a message that success can be achieved, not through industry, but, rather, via chance.*

Yet lotteries have been around for literally hundreds of years. America was created with their help. In 1612, the British crown authorized the Virginia Company of London to hold a lottery to aid the Jamestown colony. During the colonial period and after, Americans held lotteries to raise funds for internal improvements and defense. Thus how are the lotteries today different and why do they influence the traditional meaning of the American Dream?

The simple answer is advertising. State lotteries have learned the importance of effective, comprehensive marketing. Up until 1975 the federal government prohibited states from advertising, but since the ban was lifted lotteries have developed sophisticated, targeted promotions. In 1997 they spent 400 million dollars marketing the various Lotto and instant games, an amount that doubled the percentage spent on advertising by most corporations. Yet it is not merely the sheer scope of the advertising, but, rather, its effectiveness. Many critics argue that lotteries target poor groups who are least economically able to cope with the expense. In doing so, states are capitalizing on those who are perhaps most in need of realizing the American Dream. The Ohio SuperLotto game, for example, suggested in its advertising plan that "promotional 'pushes' be targeted as early as possible in the month. Government benefits, payroll and Social Security payments are released in the first Tuesday of each calendar month. This, in effect, creates millions of additional, non-taxable dollars in the local economies of which the majority is disposable." . . .

Similar to the "Millionaire" game shows, one of the key components to realizing the American Dream is luck. Once again, Americans are sent a message that success can be achieved, not through industry, but, rather, via chance. Nor have critics of the lotteries missed this phenomenon. Michael Sandel insisted that lotteries send "a message at odds with the ethic of work, sacrifice and moral responsibility. . . ." Instead, people are told that "with a little luck they can escape the world of work to which misfortune consigns them." Another critic agreed, arguing that, "in short, lotteries may undercut the ethic of work and achievement, replacing it with an ethic of luck."

Yet lotteries, in fact, do even more. They play both on the ethic of luck and attempt to fool one into believing that there is something more than luck—that skill is a component of winning. The National Gambling Impact Study Commission noted that lottery advertising specifically sought to persuade players that they could "influence their odds through the choices of numbers they pick." Moreover, there are a plethora of books that promise to teach the would-be lottery winner: *Found Money: How to Consciously Win the Lottery; The Basics of Winning Lotto-Lottery; How to Win: More Strategies for Increasing a Lottery Win*. The implication is that through hard work one can develop the skill necessary to win the lottery, and thus the American Dream.

With such a message one might argue that the American Dream is alive and well, that its integrity has been maintained. Industry, Ben Franklin's traditional ingredient, is realized through calculation and superior planning. Nothing, however, could be further from the truth. The lottery is unquestionably random. One needs only a buck, a dream, and unimaginable luck. Thus, like the "Millionaire" game shows, state lotteries, through carefully targeted advertising, have played upon and drastically altered the customary conception of the American Dream.

America's new Poor Richard mantra has become "Early to bed, early to rise, file a lawsuit and sue till they cry."

Compensation Lawsuits

If game shows and lotteries have seemingly opened a path to fulfilling the American Dream, so too has the proverbial "million dollar injury." Litigation is as American as apple pie, though it does not leave so sweet a taste in the mouth of most Americans. Indeed, many view the legal profession with disdain, especially personal injury lawyers whose ubiquitous "have you been involved in an accident? You may be entitled to compensation" advertisements encourage the public to believe that easy money can be had. Such "ambulance chasers" have spawned hundreds of lawyer jokes. "What's a million lawyers at the bottom of the sea? A good start." Such humor, though laughed off in passing, says something about the legal profession in the eyes of the public. Still, Americans file tens of thousands of lawsuits each year, many in the hopes of cashing in on a personal injury or product liability case. Some scholars have likened such strategies to playing the lottery. [For example, Jeffrey O'Connell, in *Law Suit Lottery* writes]:

> The operation of the tort system is akin to a lottery. Most crucial criteria for payment are largely controlled by chance: (1) whether one is "lucky" enough to be injured by someone whose product or conduct can be proved faulty; (2) whether the party's insurance limits or assets are sufficient to prom-

ise an award or settlement commensurate with losses and expenses; (3) whether one's own innocence of faulty conduct can be proved; and (4) whether one has the good fortune to retain a lawyer who can exploit all the variables before an impressionable jury, including graphically portraying whatever pain one has suffered.

Equating such a scenario to achieving the American Dream may be viewed as extremely strange at best. Yet the similarity between game shows, lotteries, and tort litigation is not as far-fetched as one might think. In all three situations the desired end is a trip to the bank with a fat check. In recent years a number of court cases have resulted in just such an outcome. If a plaintiff wins a lawsuit he will most likely receive not only compensatory damages (those that reimburse for medical expenses, lost wages, etc.), but may also be awarded punitive damages (those that punish the defendant for negligent or dangerous behavior). Moreover, in order to send a message to the offending company, jury awards for punitive damages often far exceed compensatory damages.

Thus like game shows and lotteries, injury and product liability lawsuits can be extremely lucrative. And once again, in such a process the traditional road to the American Dream is circumvented. Ben Franklin's industry and Lincoln's labor ethic are not components of a plaintiff's road to riches. The classic American ingredients of hard work, frugality, and self-reliance do not appear in the lawyer's brief. America's new Poor Richard mantra has become "Early to bed, early to rise, file a lawsuit and sue till they cry." . . .

The failure to take responsibility is another element that ties tort litigation to changing conceptions of the American Dream. The accident victim who causes their own injury but expects someone else to pay is very similar to the individual who believes that financial success is owed to them regardless of their lack of work ethic. In both cases, neither party accepts responsibility for their situation. Instead, they maintain a sense of entitlement that justifies their belief....

Do millionaire game shows and promises of lottery millions help to further erode the ethic of work and self-reliance that once embodied the American Dream?

The Ethics of the Evolving American Dream

The "rags to riches" legend has and continues to be a cornerstone of the American Dream. The traditional message taught that through hard work, frugality, and self-sacrifice one could achieve financial success and social mobility. Ben Franklin counseled industry, Abraham Lincoln sang the praises of the northern labor system, and Horatio Alger instilled hope in generations of Americans. All three helped to establish basic guidelines for success in a land of infinite possibility.

There are unquestionably many Americans who continue to abide by such tenets and in doing so are rewarded for their efforts. Yet there are also those who have come to believe that the American Dream's promise of riches is just that, a promise, and as such they feel entitled to instant financial success. Nor has the socio-corporate climate in America disappointed such a belief. Savvy television producers and marketing executives have latched on to the core of the American Dream. They understand that Americans are enthralled with striking it rich. Thus millionaire game shows are designed to make winning seem easy. Lotteries are marketed in such a way that one thinks they have a real shot at cashing in. The reality in both instances is that achieving the American Dream through such means is a long shot at best. Too much chance exists. Too much luck is necessary.

What is the end effect on society? Do millionaire game shows and promises of lottery millions help to further erode the ethic of work and self-reliance that once embodied the

American Dream, replacing it with an ethic of luck? Or are these sources of instant gratification merely products of an ethic already lost to some Americans? Perhaps the truth lies somewhere in the middle.

The even darker side to this cultural phenomenon is how the sense of entitlement has spilled over into a lack of responsibility. The fact that so many Americans are willing to utilize litigation to cash in on the American Dream is disheartening. Failing to take responsibility for their own mistakes, plaintiffs look to the legal system to make misfortune into fortune. Again, marketing and an avalanche of advertising by personal injury lawyers helps encourage would-be injury victims. Still, the readiness of people to sue is a key social factor.

Ultimately, most Americans would like to achieve the American Dream of financial independence. Yet it is the means to achieving it that are essential to the nation's ethical foundations. It seems that many Americans covet the easy road to the Dream and in the process undercut the core values that established the Dream in the first place. Equally culpable are the big businesses that capitalize on the quest for the Dream. In an ironic sense, such businesses are fulfilling the Dream for themselves while dangling the possibility of the Dream over the heads of the public. There can be little doubt that the producers of the millionaire games shows, the state lotteries, and lawyers are getting rich on other people's yearning for the American Dream.

2

The American Dream Does Not Exist

Lorie A. Johnson

Lorie A. Johnson calls herself a "philosopher geek" and publishes essays on her Web site Sunfell and in magazines and journals. She also works as an information systems specialist for the Arkansas state legislature.

Most people assume the American dream is about achieving the nostalgic ideal of 1950s family life—Dad in charge of the household, Mom always looking pretty, and their children happily obedient and affectionate. The belief that success means living in a suburban home with a nuclear family causes many Americans to disparage any lifestyle that departs from this false image of family life. In truth, the suburbs are full of dysfunctional families and overdeveloped housing tracts. Many people in America cannot afford to buy a home, and most families do not fit the fifties-era ideal. Nonetheless, the media and advertisers continue to promote the delusion of the American dream, and consumers continue to spend their money in hope of achieving it. However, in order to be truly happy, Americans need to reject the false American dream and create their own vision of happiness.

It is impossible to live a week in the United States and not hear something about "the American Dream." It is as much a part of our cultural mythos as is baseball, apple pie, rock-and-roll music and politics. Yet, few people really examine it closely and discover what it truly is. Is it a dream, or a vision?

Or some callously advertised ideal foisted upon us by the corporate media, cleverly disguised as our own dreams?

The middle class is vanishing, leaving home ownership to only the richest people.

The American Illusion

What is the "American Dream"? It is often presented to us as the idealistic vision of a married couple with two or more children, owning a home in the suburbs and driving one or more large cars. Everyone is solvent and well-fed, the man is king of his family, God is in His heaven and all is well with the world. It has a fifties flavor to it, this original vision—Dad in his hat, Mom in her girdled dress and pearls, and Dick and Jane with a ball and doll. Everyone knows their place and is in their places, obedient to the Dad, loving to the Mom.

When the word "family" is invoked, as it all too often is nowadays, this imaginary half-century gone domestic group is usually what is envisioned. There are no cohabiting couples, single parents, single people, elders, or people without kids. The only "true" family in the eyes of the blathering pols is this imaginary young nuclear family. No one else need apply. If you live in a rented apartment, you are a loser. If you live in the sticks, you're a hick. And don't even mention the fact that you live in a manufactured home, unless you want to be branded "trailer trash". Urban? Must be a ghetto dweller, then. No, only middle-class, Euro-descended suburbanites count. Everyone else is a mob, or worse, invisible.

What has happened to the American Dream? Why do so many people still invoke it, and worse, attempt to pursue it? Trackless rubber-stamp suburbs sprawl upon once-arable land. Instead of being little paradises, suburbs are proving to be a breeding ground for sociopaths of the sort that people still believe only live in urban cores. The houses and cars are growing like fertilized weeds and covering arable land like crabgrass to accommodate the growing girth of their inhabitants. The middle class is vanishing, leaving home ownership to only the richest people. Families today are all sorts of combinations of people. The "Brady Bunch," once considered a unique enough combination to rate a TV series of its own is now more the norm than the exception. The fifties-era family of wage-earner Dad, stay-at-home Mom, and Dick and Jane is rare, even within groups that encourage its original style—like fundamentalist Christians and orthodox Jews.

The contrast between the media-deluded "dream" and the open-eyed reality of America today is astonishing. There are no heavy people on TV, but if you look around, they are everywhere. Houses are huge on TV—not in real life. There are no gum-spotted sidewalks or weedy verges on the television. If you believed the ads on television, you'd own at least a dozen cars. And I have never seen places like what they show on TV, that are pristine and empty—instead they are overrun with crowds trying to "get away from it all" in RVs complete with satellite dishes. And to quote that Eighties song: "the sun always shines on TV."

Happiness and the reality of the American Dream are found in abandoning the false dream, and creating one of your own.

Selling the American Dream

It is difficult to resolve the difference between the media world and the real world. The difference is often jarring, especially when going to a place which tries to imitate what is shoveled out of the tube. The deliberate sleekness and marketing savvy of stores nowadays guarantees you that your shopping experience will be full of noise, flash, and every device imaginable to get you to part with your money. Malls today are carefully designed to disorient the shopper and temporarily "trap" them within their walls. This is true of grocery stores, too—where companies buy shelf space and carefully place items where certain categories of people will look. Parents get trapped into buying the heavily sugared cereal placed at the precise eye level of their young consumer target. Noise is prevalent, omnipresent, and deliberate. Entertainment stores and places that sell music and movies probably have stock in hearing aid companies, since they play the awful music they peddle at such high volumes. And even restaurants, the last bastion of civility, run at earsplitting volume. And if you are lucky enough to find a quiet, intimate place to eat, someone is sure to bring in a child who is not old enough to appreciate the food or the atmosphere and make its displeasure loudly known.

The American Dream is a delusion, an illusion meant to keep people dissatisfied and hungering to spend more money, in the hopes that the next purchase will be the one that buys them the happiness they are promised. What no one told our framers is that happiness isn't a commodity. It is something that is internal, easily found, and free of charge. Happiness and the reality of the American Dream are found in abandoning the false dream, and creating one of your own. Understanding that all the trappings of Western culture are props in a badly acted movie, and that you can throw their script away and make one of your own is a liberating experience. It is possible to have a wonderfully rich and fulfilling life without designer clothes, a wedding register, minivan, suburban house, or even a TV. In fact, turning the TV off is the first step in reclaiming your own dream.

It is a daring thing—even a little scary—*creating your own reality.* But it can be done, and is ultimately more satisfying than the fill-in-the blank blandness that our culture dictates to us. Americans were truly originals once. Now we are a whining bunch of overfed adolescents, wanting all the toys and none of the responsibility. It's time to grow up, and create a new dream. Go on—I dare you to.

3

Today's Economy Is Killing the American Dream

Robert D. Atkinson

Robert D. Atkinson is the vice president of the Progressive Policy Institute and the author of the book The Past and Future of America's Economy: Long Waves of Innovation That Power Cycles of Growth.

Today the American dream is in danger because of a growing gap between the rich and the poor. More high-wage white collar jobs and low-wage service jobs are available, but there are fewer middle-wage jobs. In addition, while the after-tax income of the wealthiest Americans is skyrocketing, the average after-tax income of the poor and middle class has risen only modestly. In order to bring the American dream within reach of all people, the government should encourage private-sector research to develop more higher-paying jobs and support labor unions that can help low-income workers earn more money. Tax policies should also aim to reduce the disparity between rich and poor.

The American dream of owning a home, buying a car, and providing economic security for one's family is a deeply held part of our psyche. But what makes America great is that this dream is not just about some people moving up, it's about all Americans moving up. Indeed, [President] Bill Clinton spoke to that core value when he said, "We need a new

Robert D. Atkinson, "Vanishing Dreams," *Blueprint Magazine*, no. 2, May 7, 2004. Reproduced by permission.

spirit of community, a sense that we are all in this together, or the American Dream will continue to wither."

Today there are troubling signs that the dream is withering.

The Growing Gap Between Rich and Poor

But today there are troubling signs that the dream is withering. Trade, technology, and other market changes appear to be hollowing out the middle class. There are a growing number of high-wage knowledge jobs and low-wage service jobs, but fewer middle-wage manufacturing and office jobs. Moreover, a growing "winner-take-all" economy means that earnings inequality is at an all-time high. The [George W.] Bush administration has exacerbated these trends with its plutocratic tax policies, making business management guru Peter Drucker's 1992 observation all the more prescient: "There is a danger that the post-capitalist society will become a class society unless service workers attain both income and dignity."

The economic data paint a bleak picture. The Congressional Budget Office recently found that the average after-tax income of the top 1 percent of the population more than doubled over this period, rising from $294,300 in 1979 to $703,100 in 2001, an increase of 139 percent (adjusted for inflation). By contrast, the average after-tax income of the households that make up the middle one-fifth of the population rose only 17 percent, while average after-tax income of the poorest one-fifth of households rose just 8 percent.

This winner-take-all phenomenon has resulted in skyrocketing income levels for those lucky enough to be in the small elite group, whether they are CEOs, entertainers, sports figures, or attorneys. The average compensation of the highest-paid CEOs went from around $5.5 million in 1970 to almost $40 million in 1999 (adjusted for inflation). The national share of wage and salary income going to the top 10 percent, 5 percent and 1 percent of taxpayers has never been higher since 1927. . . .

The Bureau of Labor Statistics (BLS) forecasts that between 2002 and 2012, jobs in the highest two wage quintiles and the lowest wage quintile will grow the fastest, with jobs in the third and fourth quintiles—the working and middle classes—will grow much more slowly. Of the 39 occupational categories where BLS predicts a loss of 5,000 or more jobs, only one, sewing machine operators, is in the lowest wage quintile. None is in the highest. In contrast, of the projected 15 fastest growing occupations, six are in the lowest quintile and three are in the highest. For example, BLS predicts that in 2012 there will be 454,000 more fast food workers making $15,150 and 376,000 more operations managers making $83,590.

There is a real risk that the U.S. economy will be increasingly made up of a growing group of high-wage knowledge workers with high incomes, and a growing group of low-wage service workers.

The Impact of Trade and Technology

Why is labor market growth looking more like a "U" than a straight line? The short answer is trade and technology. Americans have benefited from the low prices and ability to specialize in high-value-added goods and services that globalization brings. But trade has not only put downward pressure on wages in some trade-impacted sectors, it has also led to the elimination of some jobs, particularly lower-middle and middle-wage jobs. The Progressive Policy Institute calculates that, since the end of 2000, increased imports and decreased exports have contributed to the loss of more than 830,000 manufacturing jobs, with approximately 70 percent of these jobs in the second and third wage quintiles. Offshoring service jobs will only exacerbate this trend. While BLS did not factor offshoring into its predictions, projections by Forester Research of the 3.3 million jobs to be lost due to offshoring by 2015 suggest that only 10,000 will be in the lowest wage quintile; almost two-thirds will be in the middle three quintiles.

Technology plays an even bigger role than trade. Since the end of 2000, higher productivity in manufacturing was responsible for the loss of 1.1 million factory jobs and will lead to a continuing decline in the share of factory jobs. And automation is not confined to manufacturing. The rise of the digital economy is leading to a new wave of automation in the 34 million jobs involving routine processing of information. This is one reason why the number of travel agent jobs declined by 6,580 [from 2001 to 2004], as more Americans booked their own trips. It's why the BLS predicts that there will be 28,000 fewer telephone operators (average salary $29,340); 57,000 fewer secretaries ($26,390); and 93,000 fewer word processors ($27,830) in 2012.

As jobs involving routine processing of goods and information are eliminated, two broad occupational areas are likely to expand: the category of managerial, professional, and technical jobs; and service jobs in such fields as health services, child care, food preparation, and custodial services. Both types of jobs are difficult to automate—the former because they involve more complex information management and processing, and the latter because they involve providing services directly to individuals. With those occupations on the rise, there is a real risk that the U.S. economy will be increasingly made up of a growing group of high-wage knowledge workers with high incomes, and a growing group of low-wage service workers. There will be fewer and fewer middle-wage opportunities.

What should we do? Conservatives will say that there's nothing to do except perhaps prescribe even more tax cuts for the wealthy. It's their hard work, they argue, that boosts growth. Intervening, they say, rewards laziness and penalizes effort. Liberals meanwhile argue that reducing inequality is important enough to risk sacrificing growth by calling for restrictive measures, such as trade protection. New Democrats believe that high levels of income inequality are not only unfair but also a burden on economic growth. To paraphrase John Kennedy, we believe that a rising tide is needed to lift all boats, but without everyone having solid boats, a rising tide may lift yachts the highest.

Bringing the Dream Back to Life

So what should government do? First, there are things it shouldn't do. It should not try to slow down the changes brought about by trade and technological innovation, since those forces power growth. What about education? Many propose investing in all levels of education as the solvent for the corrosion of inequality. There is no doubt that investments in education will help people move to better jobs. But higher levels of educational attainment alone will not prevent educated middle-class workers from having to move into the growing number of lower-paying jobs. Education can help an individual move from being a cashier to an accountant, but alone it can't create more accountant jobs and fewer cashier jobs.

To help create more relatively good jobs, we need to take a number of steps. First, we need to put in place a national innovation agenda to help boost higher-skilled, higher-paid knowledge jobs. This means increasing federal support for research, expanding the R&D [research and development] tax credit, and boosting e-government and e-commerce, including spurring the deployment of high-speed broadband, among other things.

Public policy should also help organizations that employ workers in low-skill work environments to enrich and expand these jobs in ways that rely on workers' own knowledge and skills to create what some call "high-performance work organizations." Government can play a catalytic role by co-funding industry and union skills alliances through a new National Skills Corporation.

Reform Labor Laws

Even with these steps, there will still be a large number of low-wage jobs and high levels of income inequality. As a result, we need to take steps to ensure that the people working in them have the opportunity to do reasonably well economically. One step is to reform labor laws so unions have a fair chance to organize workers in low-wage industries and boost their incomes through collective bargaining. Another is to move decisively toward universal health coverage.

Drucker argues that making "service work productive is the first social priority of the post-capitalist society, in addition to being an economic priority." We should heed his advice. One way to do that is to help spur automation of low-wage jobs so that there are relatively more good-paying jobs relative to low-paying jobs. One factor holding back automation of low-wage jobs is precisely the fact that because they pay so little, companies have little incentive to replace cheap labor with capital. That's one reason why indexing the minimum wage to inflation makes sense, not only to raise workers' incomes but also to boost productivity. When workers make more, companies are more likely to install technology and take other steps to automate work. In addition, government R&D funds and e-commerce policy should be used to spur the development and adoption of technologies that could automate low-wage work. For example, automating toll collection and parking lot payments could reduce these low-paying, low-skill jobs. Likewise, widespread development of radio frequency identification devices on products could make it much easier for consumers to self-checkout at retail stores.

Government also needs to use tax policies to offset growing marketplace inequality, as Clinton-era policies like the

Earned Income Tax Credit did. The Bush administration tax cuts did exactly the opposite.

This means ensuring that unearned income is taxed fairly, by repealing the Bush dividends and capital gains tax cuts and adopting the Democratic proposal to reform the estate tax. It also means restoring marginal income tax rates on the wealthiest Americans to their 2000 levels.

We are at a critical juncture in our history. As the economic structure evolves in ways that increase labor market bifurcation and inequality, we can either continue on the plutocratic, laissez-faire path that the Bush administration is taking, or we can choose a path that leans into the wind of growing income inequality to bring all Americans together. The choice we make now will be felt by Americans for generations.

4

The American Dream Is Possible in Today's Economy

Barack Obama

Barack Obama serves as a U.S. senator for the state of Illinois. He has also worked as a civil rights attorney and a community activist.

Throughout American history the forces of greed and corruption have been overcome in order to ensure that all citizens have the chance to live the American dream. Today, however, rapid technological advancements and the global economy make it difficult for the poor and working classes to improve their economic status. Nonetheless, the American dream is still attainable if citizens take individual initiative and provide community support and neighborly generosity. America can still be the land of opportunity if Americans reject selfish individualism and meaningless materialism. Americans need to work together to make sure that everyone has access to the affordable education, health care, and job training needed to achieve their dreams.

[Editor's Note: The following selection is excerpted from the 2005 commencement address Barack Obama delivered at Knox College in Illinois.]

The true test of the American ideal is whether we're able to recognize our failings and then rise together to meet the challenges of our time; whether we allow ourselves to be shaped by events and history, or whether we act to shape them; whether chance of birth or circumstance decides life's big winners and losers, or whether we build a community where, at the very least, everyone has a chance to work hard, get ahead, and reach their dreams. We have faced this choice before.

Ensuring Opportunity Throughout History

At the end of the Civil War, when farmers and their families began moving into the cities to work in the big factories that were sprouting up all across America, we had to decide: Do we do nothing and allow captains of industry and robber barons to run roughshod over the economy and workers by competing to see who can pay the lowest wages at the worst working conditions? Or do we try to make the system work by setting up basic rules for the market, instituting the first public schools, busting up monopolies, letting workers organize into unions?

We chose to act, and we rose together.

When the irrational exuberance of the Roaring Twenties came crashing down with the stock market, we had to decide: Do we follow the call of leaders who would do nothing, or the call of a leader [Franklin Delano Roosevelt] who, perhaps because of his physical paralysis, refused to accept political paralysis?

We chose to act—regulating the market, putting people back to work, expanding bargaining rights to include health care and a secure retirement—and together we rose.

When World War II required the most massive homefront mobilization in history and we needed every single American to lend a hand, we had to decide: Do we listen to skeptics who told us it wasn't possible to produce that many tanks and planes? Or, did we build Roosevelt's Arsenal for Democracy and grow our economy even further by providing our returning heroes with a chance to go to college and own their own home? Again, we chose to act, and again, we rose together.

The Challenges in Today's Economy

Today, at the beginning of this young century, we have to decide again. But this time, it is your turn to choose. Here in Galesburg, [Illinois,] you know what this new challenge is. You've seen it.

All of you . . . saw what happened at 9/11. It's already been noted, the degree to which your lives will be intertwined with the war on terrorism that currently is taking place. But what you've also seen, perhaps not as spectacularly, is the fact that when you drive by the old Maytag plant around lunchtime, no one walks out anymore. I saw it during the campaign when I met union guys who worked at the plant for 20, 30 years and now wonder what they're gonna do at the age of 55 without a pension or health care; when I met the man whose son needed a new liver but because he'd been laid off, didn't know if he could afford to provide his child the care that he needed.

It's as if someone changed the rules in the middle of the game and no one bothered to tell these folks. And, in reality, the rules have changed.

It started with technology and automation that rendered entire occupations obsolete—when was the last time anybody here stood in line for the bank teller instead of going to the ATM, or talked to a switchboard operator? Then it continued when companies like Maytag were able to pick up and move their factories to some underdeveloped country where workers were a lot cheaper than they are in the United States.

Technology and Globalization

As Tom Friedman points out in his new book, *The World Is Flat*, over the last decade or so, these forces—technology and globalization—have combined like never before. So that while most of us have been paying attention to how much easier technology has made our own lives—sending e-mails back and forth on our Blackberries, surfing the Web on our cell phones, instant messaging with friends across the world—a quiet revolution has been breaking down barriers and connecting the world's economies. Now business not only has the ability to move jobs wherever there's a factory, but wherever there's an Internet connection.

Countries like India and China realized this. They understand that they no longer need to be just a source of cheap labor or cheap exports. They can compete with us on a global scale. The one resource they needed were skilled, educated workers. So they started schooling their kids earlier, longer, with a greater emphasis on math and science and technology, until their most talented students realized they don't have to come to America to have a decent life—they can stay right where they are.

The result? China is graduating four times the number of engineers that the United States is graduating. Not only are those Maytag employees competing with Chinese and Indian and Indonesian and Mexican workers, you are too. Today, accounting firms are e-mailing your tax returns to workers in India who will figure them out and send them back to you as fast as any worker in Illinois or Indiana could.

When you lose your luggage in Boston at an airport, tracking it down may involve a call to an agent in Bangalore [India], who will find it by making a phone call to Baltimore. Even the Associated Press has outsourced some of their jobs to writers all over the world who can send in a story at a click of a mouse.

As [British] Prime Minister Tony Blair has said, in this new economy, "Talent is the 21st-century wealth." If you've got the skills, you've got the education, and you have the opportunity to upgrade and improve both, you'll be able to compete and win anywhere. If not, the fall will be further and harder than it ever was before.

So what do we do about this? How does America find its way in this new, global economy? What will our place in history be?

"We're All in It Together"

Like so much of the American story, once again, we face a choice. Once again, there are those who believe that there isn't much we can do about this as a nation; that the best idea is to give everyone one big refund on their government—divvy it up by individual portions, in the form of tax breaks, hand it out, and encourage everyone to use their share to go buy their own health care, their own retirement plan, their own child care, their own education, and so on.

In Washington, they call this the Ownership Society. But in our past there has been another term for it—Social Darwinism—every man or woman for him- or herself. It's a tempting idea, because it doesn't require much thought or ingenuity. It allows us to say [to] those whose health care or tuition may rise faster than they can afford—tough luck. It allows us to say to the Maytag workers who have lost their job—life isn't fair. It lets us say to the child who was born into poverty—pull yourself up by your bootstraps. And it is especially tempting because each of us believes we will always be the winner in life's lottery, that we're the one who will be the next Donald Trump, or at least we won't be the chump who Donald Trump says: "You're fired!" to.

But there is a problem. It won't work. It ignores our history. It ignores the fact that it's been government research and investment that made the railways possible and the Internet possible. It's been the creation of a massive middle class, through decent wages and benefits and public schools that allowed us all to prosper. Our economic independence depended on individual initiative. It depended on a belief in the free market, but it has also depended on our sense of mutual regard for each other, the idea that everybody has a stake in the country, that we're all in it together and everybody's got a shot at opportunity. That's what's produced our unrivaled political stability.

And so if we do nothing in the face of globalization, more people will continue to lose their health care. Fewer kids will be able to afford the diploma you're about to receive.

More companies like United Airlines won't be able to provide pensions for their employees. And those Maytag workers will be joined in the unemployment line by any worker whose skills can be bought and sold on the global market.

Let's imagine together what we could do to give every American a fighting chance in the 21st century.

Working Together to Give Everyone a Chance

So today I'm here to tell you what most of you already know. This is not us—the option that I just mentioned. Doing nothing. It's not how our story ends—not in this country. America is a land of big dreamers and big hopes.

It is this hope that has sustained us through revolution and civil war, depression and world war, a struggle for civil and social rights and the brink of nuclear crisis. And it is because our dreamers dreamed that we have emerged from each challenge more united, more prosperous, and more admired than before.

So let's dream. Instead of doing nothing or simply defending 20th-century solutions, let's imagine together what we could do to give every American a fighting chance in the 21st century.

What if we prepared every child in America with the education and skills they need to compete in the new economy? If we made sure that college was affordable for everyone who wanted to go? If we walked up to those Maytag workers and we said "Your old job is not coming back, but a new job will be there because we're going to seriously retrain you and there's life-long education that's waiting for you"—the sorts of opportunities that Knox [College] has created with the Strong Futures scholarship program.

What if no matter where you worked or how many times you switched jobs, you had health care and a pension that stayed with you always, so you all had the flexibility to move to a better job or start a new business? What if instead of cutting budgets for research and development and science, we fueled the genius and the innovation that will lead to the new jobs and new industries of the future?

Right now, all across America, there are amazing discoveries being made. If we supported these discoveries on a national level, if we committed ourselves to investing in these possibilities, just imagine what it could do for a town like Galesburg. Ten or twenty years down the road, that old Maytag plant could re-open its doors as an ethanol refinery that turned corn into fuel. Down the street, a biotechnology research lab could open up on the cusp of discovering a cure for cancer. And across the way, a new auto company could be busy churning out electric cars. The new jobs created would be filled by American workers trained with new skills and a world-class education.

We have the talent and the resources and the brainpower.

A Tough but Rewarding Commitment

All of that is possible but none of it will come easy. Every one of us is going to have to work more, read more, train more, think more. We will have to slough off some bad habits—like driving gas guzzlers that weaken our economy and feed our enemies abroad. Our children will have to turn off the TV set once in a while and put away the video games and start hitting the books. We'll have to reform institutions, like our public schools, that were designed for an earlier time. Republicans will have to recognize our collective responsibilities, even as Democrats recognize that we have to do more than just defend old programs.

It won't be easy, but it can be done. It can be our future. We have the talent and the resources and the brainpower. But now we need the political will. We need a national commitment.

And we need each of you.

Chase the Dollar or Chase the Dream?

Now no one can force you to meet these challenges. . . .

But I hope you don't walk away from the challenge. Focusing your life solely on making a buck shows a certain poverty of ambition. It asks too little of yourself. You need to take up the challenges that we face as a nation and make them your own. Not because you have a debt to those who helped you get here, although you do have that debt. Not because you have an obligation to those who are less fortunate than you, although I do think you do have that obligation. It's primarily because you have an obligation to yourself. Because individual salvation has always depended on collective salvation. Because it's only when you hitch your wagon to something larger than yourself that you realize your true potential. . . .

The Example of Ending Slavery

Nearly two centuries ago, before civil rights, before voting rights, before Abraham Lincoln, before the Civil War, before all of that, America was stained by the sin of slavery. In the sweltering heat of southern plantations, men and women who looked like me could not escape the life of pain and servitude in which they were sold. And yet, year after year, as this moral cancer ate away at the American ideals of liberty and equality, the nation was silent.

But its people didn't stay silent for long.

One by one, abolitionists emerged to tell their fellow Americans that this would not be our place in history—that this was not the America that had captured the imagination of the world.

The resistance that they met was fierce, and some paid with their lives. But they would not be deterred, and they soon spread out across the country to fight for their cause. One man from New York went west, all the way to the prairies of Illinois to start a colony.

And here in Galesburg, freedom found a home.

Here in Galesburg, the main depot for the Underground Railroad in Illinois, escaped slaves could roam freely on the streets and take shelter in people's homes. And when their masters or the police would come for them, the people of this town would help them escape north, some literally carrying them in their arms to freedom.

Think about the risks that involved. If they were caught abetting a fugitive, [they] could've been jailed or lynched. It would have been simple for these townspeople to turn the other way; to go live their lives in a private peace. And yet, they didn't do that. Why?

My hope . . . is that . . . you decide to keep these principles alive in your own life and in the life of this country.

The Dream Is About Freedom and Equality

Because they knew that we were all Americans; that we were all brothers and sisters; the same reason that a century later, young men and women your age would take Freedom Rides down south, to work for the Civil Rights movement. The same reason that black women would walk instead of ride a bus after a long day of doing somebody else's laundry and cleaning somebody else's kitchen. Because they were marching for freedom.

Today, on this day of possibility, we stand in the shadow of a lanky, raw-boned man with little formal education who once took the stage at Old Main [Knox College's main building, site of the Lincoln-Douglas debates in 1858] and told the nation that if anyone did not believe the American principles of freedom and equality, that those principles were timeless and all-inclusive, they should go rip that page out of the Declaration of Independence.

My hope for all of you is that as you leave here today, you decide to keep these principles alive in your own life and in the life of this country. You will be tested. You won't always succeed. But know that you have it within your power to try. That generations who have come before you faced these same fears and uncertainties in their own time. And that through our collective labor, and through God's providence, and our willingness to shoulder each other's burdens, America will continue on its precious journey towards that distant horizon, and a better day.

5

Affirmative Action Ensures Equal Access to the American Dream

Philip M. Deutsch

Philip M. Deutsch, an alumnus of the Massachusetts Institute of Technology (MIT), wrote this article for MIT's student newspaper, The Tech.

Minorities have to overcome more obstacles than white Americans to achieve the American dream. The main obstacle is racism, which makes it much more difficult for minorities to gain access to the resources and opportunities that whites take for granted. Affirmative action is therefore still needed to address the social inequalities caused by racism. It is especially important that universities and colleges continue to use affirmative action in admissions in order to ensure that the next generation of leaders is educated in an environment of diversity. These leaders will not be blinded by stereotypes and racism and will be able to help eradicate the inequalities that keep the American dream out of reach for minorities.

America is the land of opportunity. If I work hard enough, I can be whatever I want to be. If I truly want something, I can get it. I will work hard and grow up to be whatever it is that makes me happy. The sky is the limit.

These statements portray the American dream. We can all remember hearing these statements and maybe even believing

Philip M. Deutsch, "The American Dream is Still Just a Dream for Most Minorities," *The Tech*, vol. 123, February 11, 2003. Reproduced by permission of the author.

them at some point in our childhood, but now they seem almost comical. If you still actually believe them, then you are either brainwashed or a wealthy white man. Simply add a few reasonable clauses to the American dream, and listen to how ridiculous it is.

The American dream seems a little more difficult to attain when the American dreaming is a member of a minority group living in poverty.

The American dream seems a little more difficult to attain when the American dreaming is a member of a minority group living in poverty. This is not to say that the dream of success and money (yes, I said success *and* money—they are not the same thing) is unattainable for certain people. It is just incredibly more difficult to achieve when one is faced with certain obstacles that others do not have to overcome.

Racial Problems Today

The truth about American society is not pretty, and the facts prove it. According to the United States Census Bureau, blacks are twice as likely to be poor compared to other races, and eight times as likely to be imprisoned. Blacks are also three times more likely to be convicted of drug violations than whites. Only 75 percent of blacks have received post–high school education, compared to 85 percent of whites. Not surprisingly, blacks on average also make less money than whites.

As of yet, black people have not been proven to possess any kind of genetic deficiency. . . . Therefore, racially speaking, there must be something wrong with our society.

What are the racial problems that exist today? Well, racism is not as strikingly obvious as it was back in the good old days, but it is still very prevalent. Have you heard of parents who don't want, or even won't allow, their child to marry someone from another race? How about all those white families flocking from a suburban town once they find out that too many minorities are moving in? Or maybe you've walked into a restaurant and seen a woman clutch her purse for dear life with eyes intensely focused on you as you pass by, simply because your skin is dark. There are several examples of racism that go on everyday, whether it's in Congress, the White House, a frat house, or the classroom.

Healing Racism

In order to achieve racial justice in our society, we need to make some drastic changes, starting with the individual citizens of this country. Most people on either side of the affirmative action argument agree that improvement of K-12 education is a major step in bringing about social equality. Racism stems from ignorance, and our greatest hope for an equal and tolerant society is continued education and racial integration starting at a young age.

Recent proposals for programs like vouchers or federal regulation of schools have tried to address educational inequalities, though it is hard to say which approach is the best way to solve this problem.

Regardless, even if we had the solution today, (which we don't) it would take years to implement on a national scale, or even longer to see the results of such a miraculous program. Until that day arrives, affirmative action is still the best way to make up for social injustices based on race, while maintaining culturally diverse college campuses across America. This diversity is especially crucial in institutions of higher education (Ivy Leagues, MIT, Stanford, etc.) where a large number of tomorrow's leaders and business executives will be in an environment with educated people from all backgrounds, helping to dispel stereotypes and racism.

Recently, a hot topic in the news has been whether affirmative action has served its purpose in providing racial equality. Allow me to bring one more interesting fact to the table to reinforce why affirmative action is still needed. A group of researchers from MIT and the University of Chicago School of Business carried out a test in order to determine whether applicants with black-sounding names received fair treatment while applying for jobs. The results were staggering.

The researchers in the study submitted 5,000 resumés to 1,250 advertisers in Boston and Chicago looking for administrative and sales help. In both cities, applicants with "white-sounding names" received 50 percent more responses from companies than their black-sounding counterparts with equal credentials.

Affirmative action acts as a part of the solution to the ongoing problem of racial injustice in our society.

Affirmative Action Makes the Dream Possible

This directly relates to affirmative action in college admissions as a way to help counteract discrimination when entering the job market. As shown in the resumé study, people do not hire based solely on merit. If companies prefer to hire whites over blacks, who knows what other minority groups might be discriminated against solely from their names and what they represent. In order to help balance the countless subtle forms of discrimination that minorities are still faced with today, giving extra advantages to the minority to counteract these unquantifiable disadvantages seems only logical. If someone goes to a slightly better school because he or she is a minority member, it will help to offset the injustices in applying for jobs (as well as other injustices), and in that respect, affirmative action will be successful.

Because we have not come up with a solution to the K-12 education system as of yet, affirmative action is necessary. Most importantly, affirmative action acts as a part of the solution to the ongoing problem of racial injustice in our society.

It is by no means the answer. Affirmative action will never fully counteract the racism and stereotyping that exists in society. However, it does, and will continue to, produce culturally aware campuses, which in turn produce culturally aware people.

6

Affirmative Action Goes Against the Spirit of the American Dream

Fritz Vaughn

Fritz Vaughn wrote this editorial for the Wake Forest University newspaper Old Gold & Black *when he was a sophomore communications and political science major. Wake Forest is in Winston-Salem, North Carolina.*

Although racial discrimination has decreased since Martin Luther King Jr. spoke of his dream of equality in 1963, minorities continue to face discrimination in the legal system and the workplace. These injustices need to be eliminated, but affirmative action or giving minorities and women preferential treatment in areas such as hiring and school admission decisions is not the right way to do this. Affirmative action insults minorities by implying they are incapable of success without special help and erodes the idea of the American dream of success through personal achievement. To restore the American dream, society must end any policies that allow preferential treatment in education and in the workplace.

I had the privilege ... to attend a prayer breakfast honoring one of this nation's greatest leaders—Dr. Martin Luther King, Jr. Throughout history, there is not a single leader I respect more than the late Dr. King. His non-violent approach to such a pressing and worthy cause in the face of numerous

Fritz Vaughn, "Affirmative Action Not the Solution to Discrimination Woes," *Old Gold & Black*, January 23, 2003. Reproduced by permission.

threats on his own life and family is especially noteworthy when coupled with the courageous, inspiring, unifying and uplifting approach he brought to the civil rights movement.

Few orations are as moving as the "I Have a Dream" speech that he delivered at the March On Washington during the summer of 1963, and no dream is as desirable as the one communicated to his followers on that hot summer day: "I have a dream that my four little children will one day live in a nation where they will not be judged by the color of their skin but by the content of their character."

Affirmative Action Hurts the Dream

It is appalling that, while we have come a long way, we have yet to fulfill this dream. The blame for this, however, cannot be laid on individual prejudices. The blame for this unjustness presently lays with the many white and black, male and female, liberal and conservative leaders who remain unwilling to lead by example; leaders who continue to turn their backs on inequality in the justice system and leaders who continue to preach affirmative action as a solution.

There is no question that minorities are discriminated against in a legal system that proclaims "equal justice for all." David Cole, a Georgetown University Law professor, reported in an article in *Champion Magazine* that the per capita incarceration rate among blacks is seven times that among whites; that while blacks make up about 12 percent of the American population, they represent more than half the prison population; and blacks serve longer prison sentences, have higher arrest and conviction rates, face higher bail amounts, and are more often the victims of police use of deadly force than [are] whites. Cole also reports that for every one African American who graduates from college, a hundred are arrested.

While I do believe that our justice system is the best in the world and generally works effectively, we are obligated to see that parts of it are reformed. Police must enforce the laws of the land equally, without clemency for any particular group of people. Judges must ensure that sentences are handed down equally, according to the crime committed and not [according to] the defendant's race or gender. The federal government and every state government must embrace a moratorium on the death penalty and assess the evenhandedness of capital punishment. As Dr. King wrote in a letter from Birmingham jail, "Injustice anywhere is a threat to justice everywhere."

We must eliminate affirmative action programs and quotas and enforce the most fundamental civil rights legislation.

Affirmative Action Demeans Minorities

Another major problem this nation faces that is just as troubling is affirmative action. The very idea of affirmative action is insulting to minorities and the American dream. While the intention appears honorable, the program is a fraudulent attempt at equality and directly contradicts Dr. King's dream that people will be judged not "by the color of their skin but by the content of their character."

U.S. Commission on Civil Rights Commissioner and the chair of the board of directors of the Center for New Black Leadership Peter Kirsanow urges the elimination of all racial classifications not justified by a compelling governmental interest, reminding us that such elimination is a fundamental law of the land. The fact of the matter is, that no matter how much spin affirmative action supporters put on the issue, affirmative action looks minorities in the face and says, "You cannot succeed without preferential treatment."

Is diversity a problem? Yes. Can racial background or gender be a merit in certain cases? Yes. But, is affirmative action the solution? No. Affirmative action is wrong, and we have been told since childhood that two wrongs do not make a right. This governmentally condoned program is both insulting and reverse discrimination in its purest form. We cannot teach the children of America's future that discrimination is wrong when our very own government discriminates.

Get Rid of Affirmative Action

While the problem of prejudice and discrimination is huge, the solution to handling it outside of educational institutions is simple. We must eliminate affirmative action programs and quotas and enforce the most fundamental civil rights legislation on the books: the Civil Rights Act of 1964 and the Voting Rights Act of 1965. These two laws encompass all civil rights violations, and if we would actually enforce them, great strides would be made.

Within educational institutions, there are two possible solutions: First, the question of race should be omitted from all applications and admittance on the basis of legacy—family history or personal ties with the university—should be banned.

The second possible solution, and most feasible since banning legacies probably would not be accepted by colleges and universities as an option, is to weigh the merits of legacy and race equally in admissions procedures.

Keeping the "dream" alive is no longer an option. It is time that we embrace the vision of Dr. Martin Luther King, Jr., and make it a reality. It is time that America becomes the very Promised Land that Dr. King spoke of in his final sermon. It is time that "Justice rolls down like waters and righteousness like a mighty stream."

7

The Dream of Home Ownership Is Still Possible

Alphonso Jackson

Alphonso Jackson is secretary of the U.S. Department of Housing and Urban Development.

In earlier times Americans dreamed of owning land. In the twentieth century, however, the American dream became that of owning a home. Federal programs in the first half of that century helped Americans become homeowners, but minority and low-income citizens were often excluded from opportunities for loans and mortgages. After the 1960s the government sought to end discrimination against disadvantaged citizens, and now more than two-thirds of Americans own homes. The current government administration has provided numerous programs to enable more families to own a home and thus fulfill the American dream.

The phrase "American Dream" has been around since historian James Adams coined it in 1931. He described it as a dream "in which each man and each woman shall be able to attain to the fullest stature of which they are innately capable, and be recognized by others for what they are, regardless of the circumstances of birth or position."

Adams gave it a name, but the idea of America as a land of unlimited possibility and opportunity has been with us since this nation's earliest days. Immigrants have been coming to our shores for nearly 400 years, searching for something better than the life they left behind.

Alphonso Jackson, "Homeownership: Myth vs. Reality," www.hud.gov, June 17, 2004. Reproduced by permission.

The wonderful thing about the American Dream is that the individual defines it. It doesn't come with a government mandate or "how to" manual. Your dream is going to be different from everyone else's. You—and only you—are its architect, builder, landlord, and tenant.

The Dream of Owning a Home

Many of these dreams have a common theme, however: the pursuit of "ownership."

At first, "ownership" meant land, and in America's early days, a person's social status was measured by the acre. But today, the pursuit is more often defined not by land itself but by what we build upon it. We don't aspire to be only landowners; we aspire to be homeowners. Homeownership and the American Dream are tied tightly together.

In the mid 1800s, miles of open land and the allure of gold drove settlers west by the tens of thousands. Many found their motivation in the Homestead Act of 1862, which promised free land to anybody who agreed to plant it and build a home. These settlers stretched the nation's borders and remade America. By the 1890s, nearly half of all Americans owned a home.

When the Great Depression struck, a quarter of the workforce lost their jobs. Homeownership slid. Banks failed. More than 40 percent of all home mortgages were in default by 1933. Lawmakers in Washington recognized that homeownership was vital to both families and the national economy. They understood that not all people were as capable of realizing the dream as others. And so the federal government made a formal commitment to expanding the ranks of homeowners.

Government Help for Aspiring Homeowners

In a flurry of activity during the 1930s, Congress and the President created the Federal Home Loan Bank System to encourage lenders to make loans to homebuyers, the Federal

Housing Administration [FHA] and FHA-insured mortgages, Fannie Mae, and public housing.

The G.I. Bill enacted during World War II stimulated homeownership by offering government-backed mortgages to veterans. But soldiers returning from the front—many of them newly married and looking for a first home—found a housing shortage instead.

Washington responded with the Housing Act of 1949, which promised "a decent home and suitable living environment for every American family." The *quality* of housing improved. The *quantity* of housing improved.

Not everyone shared in these advances, however. And so the struggle for equality in housing opportunities prompted a new assessment of the American Dream in the 1960s.

Minority and low-income citizens were being shut out. Oftentimes, they didn't have the same opportunities as others to live in the homes of their choice. Congress and the President responded with a decade of federal action intended to preserve civil rights and fairness in housing. The creation of the Department of Housing and Urban Development [HUD] in 1965 was a hallmark of the era.

Today, more than two-thirds of Americans live in homes they own. Homeownership has come to symbolize the American Dream.

Homeownership has come to symbolize the American Dream.

Homes Increase Stability

In fact, we have such a long tradition of homeownership in this country that most people don't stop to question it. Why the continued focus on homeownership? Rental housing in this country is affordable and plentiful—why don't we promote rental housing with the same enthusiasm we have for homeownership?

Rental housing has a very important place. . . . But the benefits of homeownership for families, their communities, and for the nation are simply too profound to ignore.

Owning a home is the foundation of wealth creation for families and is their quickest path to self-sufficiency. [In 2003], Americans took $139 billion out of the equity they'd accumulated in their houses and invested it in new businesses, consumer goods, their children's educations, and so on.

Homeownership offers children a stable living environment that influences their development in many positive ways. The children of homeowners score an average of 9 percent higher in math and 7 percent higher in reading ability. They're 25 percent more likely to graduate high school. They have a 116 percent better chance of graduating college.

Homeownership also provides a source of tremendous strength for the entire nation.

Over the past three years [2001-2004], the housing market has driven the national economy, as Americans bought and refinanced homes in record numbers. Many regions were spared the worst of the recent recession because the local housing market was so strong.

Today [in 2004], the housing sector directly accounts for about 14 percent of the nation's total Gross Domestic Product and involves the efforts of builders, bankers, mortgage lenders, realtors, and numerous others. For every 1,000 single-family homes built, we see 2,500 jobs created, $75 million in wages earned, and $37 million in tax revenues generated.

The robust housing market continues. As the government reported [in June 2004], housing starts remained strong in May, and building permits for single-family construction rose to their highest annual level since reporting began [in 1960].

A nation of homeowners provides stability and strength, and because we have focused so much attention throughout our history on creating better housing, America today is the best-housed nation on earth. A record number of Americans—nearly 69 percent of us—are homeowners. For the first time ever, more than half of all minority households own homes in their communities.

The reality is that owning a home is an affordable option for more families than ever before.

Can Every Family Own a Home?

Despite that success, minorities still aren't sharing equally in the homeownership dream. In fact, there's a "homeownership gap" in this country, and minority families are far less likely to own a home.

President [George W.] Bush believes that homeownership should be accessible to everyone. So he took a bold step [in 2002] and challenged the nation to close the homeownership gap and create 5.5 million new minority homeowners by the end of this decade.

I'm pleased to tell you that we're making tremendous progress. Since the President issued his homeownership challenge, more than 1.5 million minority families have taken out a mortgage on a new home.

One of the homeownership myths I want to challenge this afternoon is the idea that homeownership is unaffordable, especially for low-income families and first-time buyers who have limited means and little credit history.

The reality is that owning a home is an affordable option for more families than ever before. In many markets, a family can find a home that requires a monthly mortgage no bigger than the amount they now pay in rent. A buyer who takes time to research their options and seek out information will find countless programs on the local level dedicated to helping new consumers find a first home.

Help for Low-Income Families

The Federal Housing Administration [celebrated] its 70th anniversary [in June 2004]. Over the course of those 70 years, FHA . . . made it possible for nearly 33 million families to join the ranks of the nation's homeowners. And a person can't be denied an FHA-backed loan because they make too much money. That's another homeownership myth. If they meet the credit requirements, if they can afford the mortgage payments, and if they plan to make the property their primary residence, anyone can apply for an FHA-insured loan.

Suppose a person could afford a monthly mortgage payment, but hasn't been able to save money for a downpayment. Is homeownership out of reach for them?

The myth says yes. The reality says maybe not.

I announced recently that more than 400 state and local government agencies will share $162 million in funding through the American Dream Downpayment Initiative. These grant dollars will help first-time homebuyers with their downpayment and closing costs, which researchers tell us represent the single greatest obstacle to homeownership.

President Bush proposed the American Dream Downpayment Initiative as a candidate for the White House in 2000, and made it the centerpiece of his homeownership agenda once he took office. We worked with Congress for three years to enact it.

Now that the funds are available, we can begin helping thousands of families chart a course toward homeownership—families like the Telore family of Boston.

A Family's First House

Ramesh and Sheba Telore came to the city of Boston as immigrants from India. Ramesh became a minister at the Emmanuel Gospel Center. Sheba works as a secretary.

Sheba's great dream was to own a home, but the family couldn't manage the finances, especially a downpayment. But they took a homebuyer education course and finally had the opportunity [in 2003] to purchase a three-bedroom home in the Mission Hills area. Working through one of HUD's lending partners, they received $2,800 in downpayment and closing cost assistance, which made the home affordable.

Today, they live in a brand-new house. "It's amazing," says Ramesh in describing the family's journey to homeownership. "Our long-cherished dream has come true."

More Help for Families

Let me tell you about another innovative plan we've developed to help families jump the hurdle of high downpayments. The [Bush] Administration has proposed legislation called the Zero Down Payment Mortgage. It would allow buyers to qualify for FHA loans without having to come up with cash at the closing table. The downpayment would be rolled into the total cost of the mortgage at a slightly higher interest rate than a standard FHA loan.

We estimate that our proposal would generate 150,000 new homebuyers in the first year alone....

First-time buyers sometimes think there's nobody out there to help them navigate the process. They often don't know their rights as homebuyers. They don't fully understand their responsibilities either.

But the reality is that homeownership education is available in every large and medium-sized city in America. With the help of HUD-approved counseling agencies, families are making more informed home purchases, learning how to budget for home expenses and a regular mortgage payment, and they're finding the lending process less intimidating.

Our Administration is significantly boosting funding for housing education.... We've more than doubled the funding for housing education since 2001.

Housing Counseling

When I was with President Bush in suburban Philadelphia [in] spring [2004], we saw what housing counseling can do for a family that once considered homeownership out of reach.

For almost four years, Pearl Cerdan had been thinking about buying a home for herself and her six kids. The home-buying process always scared her off, though, and she was worried that her credit rating wasn't good enough to qualify her for a mortgage.

But Pearl heard about the services offered by a local counseling agency, and she began taking homeownership classes. She learned money-management skills, too, and how to repair her damaged credit. The counseling service helped her find low-interest financing. Soon she was signing the papers that made her a first-time homebuyer.

On March 15th [2004], Pearl greeted the President of the United States at her front door. And it was with tremendous pride that she said, "Welcome to my home." Counseling works.

We're taking many steps to help Americans become home-owners, and we're working specifically to promote the production of affordable homes. . . .

The Dream of Homeownership Is Real

America is not a perfect place, but there's perfection in her promise. It's that promise that continues to inspire people like Calloway Leffal. He turned 67 years old recently, and even though that's an age when most people start slowing down, he chose to fulfill a dream by becoming a first-time homebuyer in Dallas.

It inspires people like Carlos and Jane Arias. They came here as immigrants from Peru. They spoke no English, had no credit history, and knew nothing about the process of buying a home. Just 18 months after arriving in this country, they became proud homeowners.

And it inspires people like Kim Berry of Central Islip, New York. She's a Native American who was left without any kind of family support system when she separated from her husband and got laid off in the same year. But Kim was determined to buy a home. With the help of HUD and an entire community support system she built on her own, Kim lifted herself out of government-subsidized housing and into her own home.

It's perhaps a testament to the continuing power of homeownership that it has provoked so many myths over the years. I hope I've successfully batted down a few of them. . . . But the American Dream of homeownership itself is not a myth. From the suburbs to the inner cities, the dream of homeownership endures, and it belongs to every American.

In a great country where people are different from one another in so many ways, the American Dream is one of the strongest ties we share with one another. North to south, east to west, across all lines of ethnicity, color, religion, and gender, people share in the aspiration to own a home.

8

The Dream of Home Ownership Is Unattainable for Many Americans

Barbara J. Lipman

Barbara J. Lipman is the research director for the Center for Housing Policy and formerly served as the Housing Privatization Adviser for the U.S. Agency for International Development.

A growing number of working families are unable to afford adequate housing, and many others pay more than half of their income to secure housing for their families—well over the 30 percent of income that financial advisers recommend. The problem is that the price of housing is rising faster than are the incomes of working parents in traditionally lower-paying occupations such as retail sales, teaching, and food preparation. Furthermore, most new housing units being built are only affordable for middle- and upper-income families. In order to pay for housing, workers are increasingly sacrificing their quality of life in other areas. Families forgo adequate food, health insurance, and cars in order to live in a safe neighborhood. If nothing is done to address the housing problem, more and more families will be stuck living in overcrowded homes, unable to improve their quality of life or to achieve the American dream of owning a home.

Struggling with severe housing cost burdens is not supposed to be so commonplace. Rules of thumb help determine what families can afford. The housing industry considers housing affordable if payments are no more than 28 to 32 percent of household income. Government programs use 30 percent of income to determine how much housing assistance to give a low-income family. Financial planners advise families to spend no more than one-third of household income for housing. Yet—whether it's because jobs are lost, incomes fall, costs rise, or unforeseen circumstances—these "rules" routinely are broken. The fact is that, at last count, at least 13 million households in America pay more than *half* their income for housing and almost *4 million of these are families working full-time jobs.*

Struggling Families

For more than five years, the Center for Housing Policy ("the Center") has tracked the growing number of working families in America paying at least half of their income for housing. These families defy stereotypes. Over half are homeowners. Suburbanites outnumber city residents. They include teachers, police officers, and firefighters, as well as service workers. And while housing affordability problems are greatest in the Northeast and the West, they are growing fastest in the South and Midwest.

Housing costs, both rental and homeownership, are beyond comfortable reach for many working families.

What's more, we may be *underestimating* the extent of the problem. Housing is usually the largest and least flexible item in the family budget. How do working families that pay an excessive portion of their expenditures on housing cope? Do they cut back on food, healthcare, and other necessities? Run up a mountain of debt? Spend long hours commuting to work? And what does this all mean for the quality of life of these families, especially their children?

Why Some Working Families Pay So Much

Perhaps the first question to answer is why do so many working families face a severe housing cost burden in the first place? The Center's analysis shows that despite the "new economy," high-tech jobs are not eliminating traditional occupations that pay traditional wages. Retail sales workers, teachers, food preparation workers, cashiers, and janitors are all on the U.S. Department of Labor's list of 10 occupations with the largest projected job growth for 2002–2012. The point is large numbers of working families will continue to earn their incomes from these and other traditional occupations with similar earnings.

Meanwhile, housing costs, both rental and homeownership, are beyond comfortable reach for many working families. Nationally in 2003, in order to afford a two-bedroom apartment (using the not more than 30 percent of income rule of thumb), a worker would have had to earn $15.21 per hour. But the national median wages of a retail sales worker and a janitor were $8.82 and $8.98, respectively. In some local markets the gap is much larger.

On the homeownership side, the national median salary for licensed practical nurses of just over $33,000 was up about 4 percent between 2001 and 2003. Elementary school teachers made about $43,000, up roughly 3 percent, and police officers typically earned $45,000, up almost 7 percent. But the median-priced home was over $176,000, up more than 11 percent from 2001. This highlights a fundamental problem that even lower interest rates didn't solve: prices are not only above the level many working families can afford, but are growing faster than the incomes of these families.

At the heart of the issue is the other important reason why working families pay so much of their income for housing; namely, the lack of supply of affordable units. In a recent survey of some of the nation's largest and/or fastest growing counties, 85 percent of the county officials reported that most new housing in their counties is geared to middle- and upper-income households, not low- to moderate-income working families. A separate study of the national rental housing stock found that for the last ten years, new construction has been disproportionately concentrated in the top fifth of the rent distribution. The fact is, shortages of affordable housing confront many working families.

For some families, housing expenses may be so high that they incur hardships, such as inadequate food or drastic cutbacks in other necessities.

Families Stretched Too Thinly

Spending half their income on housing—the definition of a severe housing cost burden—leaves less left over for everything else, diminishing the quality of life of working families and their children. While that argument seems logical, the story is more complicated. In some respects, half of income is as arbitrary a standard as 30 percent. For example, a household with an income of $80,000 paying half for housing would have $40,000 left over for everything else. But a household spending 30 percent of $22,000 (roughly the equivalent of two minimum wages) would have only $15,400 left for meeting other needs.

Family size matters, too. A single person with the same $22,000 and spending 50 percent of income on housing ($916 per month) would have $916 left over each month to devote to other necessities. But a three-person household with the same income would have only $306 per person to meet other needs.

Of course, there is some truth to the adage that "a dollar can only be stretched so far." For some families, housing expenses may be so high that they incur hardships, such as inadequate food or drastic cutbacks in other necessities. Even when parents try to protect their children, by skimping on food so their children don't go without, for example, the resulting problems for parents, such as depression, place children at higher risk for health and psychological problems.

Some families, however, may *choose* to spend a large portion of their income on housing to live in a "better" home or neighborhood for their children—benefits they believe outweigh the difficulty of having less money available for everything else. Research studies show what many of these parents already know firsthand: Bad home environments can put young children and adolescents at risk, while a "good quality" neighborhood can lead to good outcomes, including higher income later in life. Homeowners, particularly, may see benefits in making the sacrifice. They obtain both a valuable asset and a tax break in the process. And a number of research studies link homeownership with higher levels of child well-being. However, if in the course of achieving these goals parents are foregoing important items like healthcare, savings, or pensions, they may be jeopardizing their own futures.

In short, paying an excessive portion of their income for housing is a constraint for some working families and a choice—albeit a difficult one—for others. Moreover, there are quality of life decisions working families make to *avoid* paying so much of their income for housing. Crowding into housing and making inordinately long commutes are two common ways to cope with high housing costs, but these strategies entail costs of their own. . . .

High housing costs have negative consequences for the quality of life for working families

---

Making Sacrifices

This research looked at the expenditures of low- to moderate-income working families that have severe housing cost burdens. If they are spending so much of their income on housing, are they cutting back in other ways that could negatively affect their quality of life? This study found some evidence of that, especially in the "discretionary" areas of food, healthcare, and health insurance. After meeting their housing costs, renters are more likely to have too few dollars available for food or adequate healthcare. But the major tradeoff, for both homeowners and renters is for transportation.

Our analysis showed that working families living in relatively affordable housing (i.e., accounting for 30 percent or less of household expenditures) spent on average 24 percent of their total expenditures on transportation. By contrast, families spending more than half of their total household expenses on housing spent a considerably less 7.5 percent of their total outlays on transportation. Moreover, the analysis shows a clear tradeoff between housing costs and transportation that is both statistically and economically significant (about 77 cents for every dollar decrease in housing costs).

While there is evidence of tradeoff between housing and transportation, both are typically the most expensive items in the household budget. When both are taken into account, the number of working families with a critical affordability problem increases five-fold from 8.3 percent to 44.3 percent of all working families.

Many working families will stay mired in this situation to be joined by growing numbers of other families in similar circumstances.

Together, these findings suggest that some working families are unable to locate affordable housing closer to where they work and must, therefore, trade off housing costs for commuting costs. They also suggest other ways high housing costs have negative consequences for the quality of life for working families—commuting affects for the worse their money, their time, and even the environment in which they live. . . .

Material Hardships

Material hardships are more common among working families that pay more than half their income for housing than among those who do not. Among these hardships are food insecurity, lack of health insurance, lack of a car, and—to the extent it is used as a strategy to cope with high housing costs—the physical and emotional discomforts of crowding. These are clearly more common among working families that spend more of their income on housing because these families have less to spend on other necessities. As noted in the expenditure analyses in the previous section of this report, renters are among those most likely to make these compromises. Of particular concern is the fact that the presence of children increases the risk that a family will pay high housing costs and endure hardships.

Low income and education levels are the common characteristics of working families that both pay half their income for housing and endure these hardships. In the future, unless incomes gain substantial ground against rising housing costs or more affordable housing geared to these families is produced, many working families will stay mired in this situation to be joined by growing numbers of other families in similar circumstances.

While there is a strong and consistent association between paying half of income for housing and material hardships, the connection between paying half of income for housing and child and adult well-being is more complex. Whether paying more than half their income for housing bodes well or ill for adults and children in working families depends on other factors such as family income and neighborhood quality. These

factors, in turn, bear on whether working families have a critical housing affordability problem in the first place.

This study was a first foray into the topic using data that
are not traditionally used to address housing issues. Clearly
much more needs to be done to better understand the link
between the cost of housing and the quality of life of working
families.

9

Immigration Keeps the American Dream Alive

Rupert Murdoch

Rupert Murdoch is chairman and chief executive of News Corporation.

In the aftermath of the 9/11 terrorist attacks, it is easy to fear and disparage immigrants coming to American shores. Immigrants are blamed for threatening security and burdening the economy. In truth, many immigrants serve in the armed forces along with native-born Americans, dedicating their lives to protecting the country's borders and preserving American liberty. Contrary to common assumptions, immigrant children tend to be high achievers in schools and colleges. More often than not, it is immigrant entrepreneurs and workers who demonstrate the spirit of the American dream by realizing their goals through hard work and perseverance.

[Editor's Note: The following selection is an excerpt from an acceptance speech Rupert Murdoch delivered upon receiving the 2004 B.C. Forbes Award.]

When B.C. Forbes sailed for America from Scotland in 1904, he was following a course well worn by generations of Scots.

I know how the founder of *Forbes* magazine must have felt. The Murdochs originally hail from the same part of Scotland. Today, we are part of the most recent wave of immigrants attracted by the bright beacon of American liberty.

These days, it's not always easy to talk about the benefits of immigration. Especially since 9/11, many Americans worry about borders and security. These are legitimate concerns. But surely a nation as great as America has the wit and resources to distinguish between those who come here to destroy the American Dream—and the many millions more who come to live it.

Anyone who comes here and gives an honest day's work for an honest day's pay is not only putting himself closer to the American Dream, he's helping the rest of us get there too.

Immigrant Achievements

The evidence of the contributions these immigrants make to our society is all around us—especially in the critical area of education. [Economist] Adam Smith (another Scotsman) knew that without a decent system of education, a modern capitalist society was committing suicide. Well, our modern public school systems simply are not producing the talent the American economy needs to compete in the future. And it often seems that it is our immigrants who are holding the whole thing up.

In a study on high school students released this past summer [2004], the National Foundation for American Policy found 60% of the top science students, and 65% of the top math students, are children of immigrants. The same study found that seven of the top award winners at the 2004 Intel Science Talent Search were immigrants or children of immigrants. This correlates with other findings that more than half of engineers—and 45% of math and computer scientists—with Ph.D.s now working in the U.S. are foreign born.

It's not just the statistics. You see it at our most elite college and university campuses, where Asian immigrants or their children are disproportionately represented. And a recent study of 28 prestigious American universities by researchers from Princeton and the University of Pennsylvania found something startling: that 41% of the black students attending these schools described themselves as either immigrants or children of immigrants.

The point is that by almost any measure of educational excellence you choose, if you're in America you're going to find immigrants or their children at the top. I don't just mean engineers and scientists and technicians. In my book, anyone who comes here and gives an honest day's work for an honest day's pay is not only putting himself closer to the American Dream, he's helping the rest of us get there too.

Ordinary Heroes

As Ronald Reagan said at the Statue of Liberty, "While we applaud those immigrants who stand out, whose contributions are easily discerned, we know that America's heroes are also those whose names are remembered by only a few."

Let me share some of these names with you.

Start with Eddie Chin, an ethnic Chinese Marine who was born a week after his family fled Burma. You've all seen Cpl. Chin. Because when Baghdad fell, he was the Marine we all watched shimmy up the statue of Saddam Hussein to attach the cable that would pull it down.

Or Lance Cpl. Ahmad Ibrahim. His family came to the U.S. from Syria when the first Gulf War broke out. Now Cpl. Ibrahim hopes to be deployed to Iraq—also as a Marine—to put his Arabic language skills in the service of Corps and Country.

Or what about Cpl. José Gutierrez, who was raised in Guatemala and came to America as a boy—illegally! Cpl. Gutierrez was one of the first Marines killed in action in Iraq.

As his family told reporters, this young immigrant enlisted with the Marine Corps because he wanted to "give back" to America.

So here we have it—Asian Marines, Arab Marines, Latino Marines—all united in the mission of protecting the rest of us. Isn't this what Reagan meant when he said that the bond that ties our immigrants together—what makes us a nation instead of a collection of individuals—is "an abiding love of liberty"? So the next time you hear people whining about what a "drain" on America our immigrants are, it might be worth asking if they consider these Marines a drain.

It is America's immigrants who remind us—by dint of their success—that the Dream is alive, and well within reach.

Immigrants Keep the Dream Alive

Maybe this is more clear to businessmen because of what we see every day. My company, News Corporation, is a multinational company based in America. Our diversity is based on talent, cooperation and ability.

Frankly it doesn't bother me in the least that millions of people are attracted to our shores. What we should worry about is the day they no longer find these shores attractive. In an era when too many of our pundits declare that the American Dream is a fraud, it is America's immigrants who remind us—by dint of their success—that the Dream is alive, and well within reach of anyone willing to work for it. . . .

The immigrant editor B.C. Forbes spent much of the 20th century championing the glories of American opportunity. We who have arrived more recently likewise will never forget our debt we owe to this land—and the obligation to keep that same opportunity alive in the 21st.

10

Immigration Destroys the American Dream

John C. Vinson

John C. Vinson is the editor of the Americans for Immigration Control Newsletter.

For most Americans, the American dream is about living peacefully in a community that shares a common culture. Americans have always cherished the freedom to pursue individual success, but they have also balanced that individualism with social mores that foster harmony and a sense of belonging among their likeminded neighbors. When foreigners move into American communities, they bring with them behaviors and values that do not mesh with the American way of life. Cultural conflicts that result from immigration destroy the ability of working Americans to live in harmony, advance materially, and improve their communities. People who promote immigration tend to be cultural elites who can afford to live in homogeneous neighborhoods. They do not deal directly with the problems caused by cultural diversity. Some immigration advocates even benefit from the racial antagonism they encourage because they claim they are the only ones who can mediate racial tensions. The truth is that those who oppose immigration are not bigots; they are simply expressing their desire to preserve the common dream of ordinary Americans.

John C. Vinson, "It's Righteous Indignation, Not Hate," *Americans for Immigration Control Newsletter*, 2005. © 2005 Americans for Immigration Control. Reproduced by permission.

Many Americans object when immigration changes their neighborhoods and communities beyond recognition. When they do, they can count on swift criticism from immigration enthusiasts, who are quick to label their reaction as "fear" and "hate." The proper response, say these moralists, is to "celebrate" the new diversity of peoples, nearly all of whom are "hard-working" folk who just want "the American dream." Wanting a common culture, they piously intone, is "bigotry."

Is it really? To be sure, many Americans in the newly "diverse" areas show anger, though just as many, quite often, are more sad than mad. But is anger in such cases inappropriate, or even immoral? The answer most certainly is no—at least if common sense has any say-so on the matter.

Even when immigrants are hard-working, this does not mean that they share all American values and sentiments.

Human Nature Prefers Familiarity

Like it or not, people generally prefer the familiar. Human beings, by their nature, desire a sense of belonging, and belonging requires common values. This is not irrational prejudice, but rational practicality. Though diversity may be enjoyable for a vacation, the work-a-day world works best when common ties keep social friction to a minimum.

Agreed-upon standards and values, derived from Western culture, have been the source of American success and freedom. Communities of Americans, working in harmony, have achieved impressive civic and material goals without needing government as a rule-maker and a referee for their activities.

Sadly this harmony is fading, as community after community falls victim to the kind of diversity which destroys common purpose. Even when immigrants are hard-working, this does not mean that they share all American values and sentiments. To illustrate, the August 1998 issue of *National Geographic* ran a generally pro-immigration article about New York's Chinatown. It noted the work ethic of recent Chinese immigrants. The author commented, however, that all [whom] he met "[used] the same word for [American] white people. It means 'barbarian.'"

Cultural Chaos

If the numbers of newcomers in a community are sufficiently large, a clash of cultures—and confusion—will follow. Many natives, feeling like foreigners in their own country, will experience a deep sense of alienation, a psychological condition characterized by anger and sadness. Such anger is entirely appropriate, and is justified further by the undemocratic manner through which "diversity" comes about. Politicians often show no appreciation of their constituents' feelings toward immigration, or if they do they lie about the consequences. A classic example was Sen. Ted Kennedy's promise in 1965 that the immigration act of that year would not cause "our cities [to be filled] with a million immigrants annually," or change the country's make-up.

> *Backers of mass-immigration may posture all they like about the 'American dream.' For patriotic citizens, their dream is the American nightmare.*

Why then do diversity advocates want to inflict cultural pandemonium on their fellow citizens? Aside from monetary and political gain, two other explanations are ignorance and treachery. Many elitists favor diversity because they seldom see it in full-blown form. Almost as ironclad as a law of physics is the principle that support for diversity increases in direct proportion to the distance from it.

American Dream Hypocrites

To economic elites, diversity is the pleasant experience of eating out at some tony ethnic restaurant. Afterwards, commonly, they return home to up-scale homogenous neighborhoods where no one plays loud foreign music all night long or butchers goats in the back yard. Cultural enrichments like these are left to the American masses, along with such amenities as schools where their children are shortchanged because of bilingualism and other immigration-induced fads.

On the treachery side are neo-Marxists in foundations and universities who welcome an alienated and balkanized society. Their network is well-documented in William Hawkins' book, *Importing Revolution*. Flying the banner of "political correctness," they see themselves as the lords of enlightenment who should properly rule society. When society falls apart, they stand ready to offer their services as mediators and "managers of diversity."

It is ironic that these types are the first to cry "racism" when challenged. In point of fact, racial antagonism benefits their agenda perfectly, which is why they promote mass immigration and the inevitable misunderstandings it brings.

Most ironic too is how the pro-immigration side constantly harps on the issue of "compassion." This, they tell us, is what Americans owe all comers. Yet no such empathy is ever available for the heart-felt anguish of patriotic citizens, native and foreign-born, who mourn the incremental loss of their country and way of life. The anger they feel is not hate, but righteous indignation, which they have the right—and indeed the duty—to express. Backers of mass-immigration may posture all they like about the "American dream." For patriotic citizens, their dream is the American nightmare.

Immigrants Face Barriers in Realizing the American Dream

Patricia Maldonado, Maria Rodriguez, Priya Sampath, and Elizabeth Tracy

Patricia Maldonado, Priya Sampath, and Elizabeth Tracy are staff members of the Human Services Coalition of Dade County, a Florida organization that promotes civic engagement, economic fairness, and access to health and human services. Maria Rodriguez is the coordinator of the Florida Immigrant Coalition, which fights for the fair treatment of immigrants.

Immigration can contribute greatly to national and local economies, but immigrants often have to overcome difficult hurdles to achieve the American dream. Since the terrorist attacks of September 11, 2001, some immigrants have been unable to get driver's licenses, a necessary form of identification for finding employment. In addition, while many immigrants want to go to college, many cannot afford to because they do not qualify for in-state tuition. Immigrants also tend to earn very low wages, making it difficult for families to achieve financial stability and the American dream.

Immigrants play an important role in our nation, as workers, as entrepreneurs, as taxpayers. Many achieve success, attain the "American Dream" and become donors and civic leaders. Given their growing numbers, especially in South Florida, immigrants, with strong community support, will play an even more crucial role in the future vitality of our country and economy.

Patricia Maldonado, Maria Rodriguez, Priya Sampath and Elizabeth Tracy, "Immigration and Jobs in Our Community," Human Services Coalition of Dade County, 2005. Reproduced by permission.

Immigrants represent one in eight workers in the United States, adding $10 billion to the economy each year, according to a 1997 study by the National Academy of Sciences. Most arrive to the United States in their prime working years. However, 43 percent of immigrant and 44 percent of refugee families with full-time workers have incomes below 200 percent of the federal poverty level ($37,700 for a family of four). Of the population growth in Miami-Dade, two-thirds is attributed to immigrant migration. According to *Demographic Profile Miami-Dade County Florida, 1960–2000*, in 2000, 51% of those living in Miami-Dade County were foreign born. . . .

Many Americans worry that the growing number of immigrants in their community will be a drain on government resources.

Many immigrants go on to own businesses and participate in their new community, running for political office and showing up to the polls in record numbers on Election Day. They create thriving neighborhoods with vibrant business districts much like Chinatown in New York City or Little Havana in Miami.

But that transition from immigrant to productive resident is a difficult one. Not only has achieving residency become more difficult since 9/11, many Americans worry that the growing number of immigrants in their community will be a drain on government resources.

Immigrants' Access to Driver's Licenses

The U.S. Congress and state legislatures recently have considered and implemented measures to restrict immigrants' access to driver's licenses. These proposals go well beyond denying undocumented immigrants access to driver's licenses and are likely to affect legal immigrants and even U.S. citizens. These laws are intended to increase national security; however they may interfere with effective law enforcement. Representative Jeff Flake (R-AZ) introduced H.R. 4043 in March of 2002.[1] This measure would bar federal agencies from accepting the following for identification purposes: state-issued driver's license or other comparable identification document, unless the state requires that such licenses or documents issued to non-immigrant aliens expire upon the expiration of the aliens' nonimmigrant visa.

Some state officials have linked the denial of driver's licenses to undocumented immigrants to efforts to combat terrorism. They allege that the driver's licenses that several of the terrorists [who perpetrated the 9/11 attacks] obtained facilitated their activities.

At the same time, some state officials have linked the denial of driver's licenses to undocumented immigrants to efforts to combat terrorism, alleging that the driver's licenses that several of the terrorists obtained facilitated their activities. Since [the attacks of] September 11, many states are considering proposals to tighten the rules regarding driver's license eligibility and to further restrict immigrants' access to driver's licenses.

However, some would argue the contrary in terms of public safety. The terrorists did not need U.S.-issued driver's licenses to board planes on September 11. They had foreign passports that would have enabled them to board. In fact, it was through the driver's license records that the September 11 assailants were identified. Some argue that the issuance of driver's licenses provide some control and information of who is actually in the country. Others claim that the denial of drivers license to undocumented immigrants poses a public safety

---

1. The measure passed a Committee on the Judiciary subcommittee in May 2002, but received no further consideration after that.

threat, as there are so many who are driving unlicensed, further aggravating the high numbers of uninsured drivers in the state. Although initial research and surveys of car dealerships and insurance brokers are not yet definitive, it is suspected that these industries are detrimentally affected by this policy.

Unable to Afford a College Education

Florida state colleges and universities charge a different tuition for Florida residents and non-Florida residents. For example, the University of Florida charges $2,630 for state resident students (in-state) and $12,096 for non-Florida (out-of-state) residents. Though in-state tuition is stated as the rate for state resident students, many state resident students are excluded from this rate because of their immigration status. Undocumented immigrant college students in Florida must pay out-of-state tuition to attend state colleges and universities. Federal law guarantees the right of all students, regardless of immigration status, to a high school education. Throughout the country the policies regarding residency requirements vary greatly. Some states define [the] residency requirement as simply "physical presence and intent to stay." Others, like Florida, require students to have INS (Department of Homeland Security) authorization.

Immigrants, particularly undocumented immigrants, are more likely to receive low wages.

Current Florida policy prohibits undocumented immigrant students to pay in-state post-secondary tuition even if they have been residents of Florida for many years. If changed, Florida universities and community colleges would likely enroll a few thousand new students yearly. The addition of these new students would add $1 to $2 million dollars in tuition payments. There is a possibility of some tuition loss from a small number of current students paying out-of-state tuition who would newly qualify for the in-state rate. Some people believe that these rules undermine the ability of this population to prepare to fully participate and contribute to the life of the community.

Most Immigrants Earn Little Income

Tourism and agriculture are two of the major industries that contribute to the economy of Florida. The citrus and decorative plant industries alone contribute millions to our state. Both these sectors rely heavily on the low-wage immigrant labor force. Immigrants, particularly undocumented immigrants, are more likely to receive low wages. It is estimated that the average annual salary of a farmworker family is $7,000 per year.

Some groups argue that immigrant workers take jobs away from U.S. citizens. Others respond that these industries are profitable precisely because of the low-paid immigrant labor. Proponents of legalization state that their undocumented status makes them vulnerable to exploitation and lowers the wage floor across the board.

Organizations to Contact

American Alliance for Rights and Responsibilities (AARR)
1725 K St. NW, Suite 1112, Washington, DC   20006
(202) 785-7844 • fax: (202) 785-4370

AARR believes that democracy can work only if the defense of individual rights is matched by a commitment to individual and social responsibility. It is dedicated to restoring the balance between rights and responsibilities in American life. It publishes the bimonthly newsletter *Rights and Responsibilities.*

American Center for Law and Justice (ACLJ)
PO Box 64429, Virginia Beach, VA   23467
(757) 226-2489 • fax: (757) 226-2836
Web site: www.aclj.org

The center is a public interest law firm and educational organization dedicated to promoting liberty, life, and the family. ACLJ provides legal services and support to attorneys and others who are involved in defending the religious and civil liberties of Americans. It publishes the booklets *Students' Rights and the Public Schools* and *Taking the Gospel to the Streets: Your Rights to Preach the Good News in Public Places.*

American Civil Liberties Union (ACLU)
125 Broad St., 18th Fl., New York, NY   10004
(212) 549-2500 • fax: (212) 549-2646
Web site: www.aclu.org

The ACLU is a national organization that works to defend Americans' civil rights as guaranteed by the U.S. Constitution and to establish people's equality before the law, regardless of race, color, sexual orientation, or national origin. The ACLU publishes and distributes policy statements, pamphlets, and the semiannual newsletter *Civil Liberties Alert.*

American Dream Coalition
PO Box 1590, Bandon, OR   97411
(541) 347-1517 • fax: (305) 422-0379
Web site: http://americandreamcoalition.org

The American Dream Coalition is an organization that works to decrease regulations and restrictions that limit affordable housing, transportation mobility, and economic free will. Deregulation, the organization believes, is essential to preserving the American dream. The coalition holds an annual Preserving the American Dream conference, provides leadership training, and monitors federal agency programs. Its publications, available on its Web site, include the *Guide to the American Dream* CD-ROM collection of conference papers and presentations.

American Dreams Foundation
3950 Koval La., #3029, Las Vegas, NV   89109
(702) 732-1971 • fax: (702) 732-2815
Web site: www.usdreams.com

The purpose of the American Dreams Foundation is to help provide positive educational resources that inspire and motivate America's youth and future leaders to reach for their dreams. The nonprofit foundation's Web site was developed by Jim Bickford, author of *The American Dreams Collection* and a motivational speaker about the American dream. The site offers a series of letters by people who have achieved the American dream.

American Vision
3150A Florence Rd. SW, Ste. 2, Powder Springs, GA   30127
(770) 222-7266 • fax: (770) 222-7269
Web site: www.americanvision.org

American Vision is a Christian educational organization working to build a Christian civilization. It believes the Bible ought to be applied to every area of life, including government. American Vision publishes the monthly newsletter *Biblical Worldview*.

Cato Institute
1000 Massachusetts Ave. NW, Washington, DC 20001-5403
(202) 842-0200 • fax: (202) 842-3490
Web site: www.cato.org

The Cato Institute is a libertarian public policy research foundation dedicated to limiting the control of government and protecting individual liberties. It offers numerous publications on public policy issues, including the triennial *Cato Journal*, the bimonthly newsletter *Cato Policy Report*, and the quarterly magazine *Regulation*.

The Center for a New American Dream
6930 Carroll Ave., Ste. 900, Takoma Park, MD 20912
(301) 891-3683; toll-free: (877) 68-DREAM
Web site: www.newdream.org

The Center for a New American Dream provides educational materials to help individuals, institutions, communities, and businesses to conserve natural resources and consume responsibly to protect the environment, enhance quality of life for all Americans, and promote social justice. The center provides books, videos, petitions, organizing events, and a quarterly newsletter titled *In Balance*.

Christian Coalition
1801-L Sara Dr., Chesapeake, VA 23320
(804) 424-2630 • fax: (804) 434-9068
Web site: www.cc.org

Founded by evangelist Pat Robertson, the coalition is a grassroots political organization of Christian fundamentalists working to stop what it believes is the moral decay of government. The coalition seeks to elect moral legislators and opposes extramarital sex and comprehensive drug and sex education. Its publications include the monthly newsletter *Religious Right Watch* and the monthly tabloid *Christian American*.

Coalition on Human Needs

1700 K St. NW, Ste. 1150, Washington, DC   20006
(202) 736-5885 • fax (202) 785-0791
Web site: www.chn.org

The coalition is a federal advocacy organization concerned with federal budget and tax policy, housing, education, health care, and public assistance. It lobbies for adequate federal funding for welfare, Medicaid, and other social services. Its publications include *How the Poor Would Remedy Poverty* and the bimonthly newsletter *Insight/Action*.

The Heritage Foundation

214 Massachusetts Ave. NE, Washington, DC   20002-4999
(202) 546-4400
toll-free: (800) 544-4843 • fax: (202) 544-6979
Web site: www.heritage.org

The Heritage Foundation is a conservative public policy research institute that advocates free-market economics and limited government. Its publications include the monthly *Policy Review*, the Backgrounder series of occasional papers, and the Heritage Lectures series.

Institute for Alternative Futures (IAF)

100 N. Pitt St., Ste. 235, Alexandria, VA   22314
(703) 684-5880 • fax: (703) 684-0640
Web site: www.altfutures.com

The institute consults with, and provides speakers to, various organizations concerned with health futures, information futures, and business and community futures. Books published by IAF include *Mending the Earth: A World for Our Grandchildren* (1990), *Regulating Change: The Regulation of Foods, Drugs, Medical Devices, and Cosmetics in the 1990s* (1990), and *20-20 Visions: Health Care Information, Standards, and Technologies* (1993).

The Library of Congress

101 Independence Ave. SE, Washington, DC   20540

(202) 707-5000

Web site: www.loc.gov

The Library of Congress is the federal library that serves as the research arm of the U.S. Congress. It is the largest library in the world and provides free access to written documents, sound recordings, photographs, films, maps, and sheet music that document the American experience. In 1990 the library began to digitize its collections under the American Memory project, and more than 5 million historical treasures became available to the public on the World Wide Web by 2000.

People for the American Way (PFAW)

2000 M St. NW, Ste. 400, Washington, DC   20036

(202) 467-4999 • fax: (202) 293-2672

Web site: www.pfaw.org

PFAW works to increase tolerance and respect for America's diverse cultures, religions, and values such as freedom of expression. It distributes educational materials, leaflets, and brochures and publishes the quarterly *Press Clips*, a collection of newspaper articles concerning censorship.

Progressive Policy Institute (PPI)

600 Pennsylvania Ave. SE, Ste. 400, Washington, DC   20003

(202) 546-0007 • fax: (202) 544-5014

Web site: www.dlcppi.org

PPI is a public policy research organization that strives to develop alternatives to the traditional debate between liberals and conservatives. It advocates economic policies designed to stimulate broad upward mobility and social policies designed to liberate the poor from poverty and dependence. The institute publishes the book *Building the Bridge: 10 Big Ideas to Transform America*.

Puerto Rico and the American Dream
161 E. 106th St., New York, NY   10029
(212) 828-0401 • fax: (212) 828-0402
Web site: www.prdream.com

Puerto Rico and the American Dream is the award-winning Web site on the history, culture, and politics of Puerto Rico and of Puerto Ricans who have immigrated to the United States. Founded in 1999, this multimedia site brings original content online in Spanish and English. A film section, an online gallery, discussion boards, historical timelines, and oral histories are featured along with announcements and current events postings.

Stanford Research International
333 Ravenswood Ave., Menlo Park, CA   94025
(415) 326-6200 • fax: (415) 326-5512
Web site: www.sri.com

Stanford Research International is a nonprofit research and consulting firm whose objectives are to assist public and private organizations with research and consulting services and to be a source of future perspectives for business and government. It publishes the books *American Social Trends* (1989), *The Power of Strategic Vision* (1991), *Visioning (and Preparing for) the Future* (1991), and *Rewriting the Corporate Social Charter* (1992).

The Urban Institute
2100 M St. NW, Washington, DC   20037
(202) 833-7200 • fax: (202) 223-3043
Web site: www.urban.org

The institute is a nonprofit public policy research foundation. It investigates social and economic problems confronting the nation and assesses government policies and public and private programs designed to alleviate such problems. Its publications include the periodicals *Policy and Research Report, Policy Bites,* and *Update.*

White House Kids
The White House, Washington, DC   20500
(202) 456-1111 • fax: (202) 456-2461
Web site: www.whitehouse.gov/kids

As the residence of the president of the United States, the White House provides a Web site for youth to access information about American history and to promote American patriotism. Resources include the White House Dream Team, a set of biographies about Americans who have achieved the American dream. Youth can also take a virtual tour of the White House, learn about the pets of American presidents, and view holiday celebrations in Washington, D.C.

Bibliography

Books

William A.V. Clark	*Immigrants and the American Dream: Remaking the Middle Class.* New York: Guilford, 2003.
Jim Cullen	*The American Dream: A Short History of an Idea That Shaped a Nation.* New York: Oxford University Press, 2003.
Jason DeParle	*American Dream: Three Women, Ten Kids, and a Nation's Drive to End Welfare.* New York: Penguin, 2005.
Barbara Ehrenreich	*Bait and Switch: The (Futile) Pursuit of the American Dream.* New York: Metropolitan, 2005.
Barbara Ehrenreich	*Nickel and Dimed: On (Not) Getting By in America.* New York: Owl, 2002.
Alan Elliot	*A Daily Dose of the American Dream: Stories of Success, Triumph, and Inspiration.* Nashville: Rutledge Hill, 1998.
Dolores Hayden	*Redesigning the American Dream: Gender, Housing, and Family Life.* New York: Norton, 2002.
Bob Herbert	*Promises Betrayed: Waking Up from the American Dream.* New York: Times Books, 2005.

Jennifer L. Hochschild and Nathan Scovronick

The American Dream and the Public Schools. New York: Oxford University Press, 2004.

Cal Jillson

Pursuing the American Dream: Opportunity and Exclusion over Four Centuries. Lawrence: University Press of Kansas, 2004.

Anatol Lieven

America Right or Wrong: An Anatomy of American Nationalism. New York: Oxford University Press, 2004.

Michelle Miller-Adams

Owning Up: Poverty, Assets, and the American Dream. Washington, DC: Brookings Institution, 2002.

Mark Nepo, ed.

Deepening the American Dream: Reflections on the Inner Life and Spirit of Democracy. San Francisco: Jossey-Bass, 2005.

Kyeyoung Park

The Korean American Dream: Immigrants and Small Business in New York City. Ithaca, NY: Cornell University Press, 1997.

David K. Shipler

The Working Poor: Invisible in America. New York: Vintage, 2005.

Paul Stiles

Is the American Dream Killing You? How "the Market" Rules Our Lives. New York: Collins, 2005.

Studs Terkel

American Dreams: Lost and Found. New York: New Press, 1999.

Helen Zia	*Asian American Dreams: The Emergence of an American People.* New York: Farrar, Straus & Giroux, 2001.

Periodicals

Chris Bachelder, Julia Klien, and Jim Rossi	"The Jungle at 100," *Mother Jones*, January/February 2006.
Stephanie Clifford	"Cracks in the Melting Pot," *Inc.*, December 2005.
Manohla Dargis	"Stranded on the Flip Side of the American Dream," *New York Times*, December 21, 2005.
Barbara Ehrenreich	"A Storm of Greed," *Progressive*, January 2006.
Linda Feldmann	"The Fractious Politics of Immigration," *Christian Science Monitor*, December 1, 2005.
Jason Fleming and Janelle Fleming	"Can Young 'Dream-Seekers' Avoid Being Strapped by Debt?" *Christian Science Monitor*, January 23, 2006.
Marilyn Gardner	"Her American Dream," *Christian Science Monitor*, March 7, 2005.
Marilyn Gardner	"Why Can't Money and Women Get Along?" *Christian Science Monitor*, January 31, 2006.
Jeffrey Goldberg	"The Believer," *New Yorker*, February 13, 2006.

Brian Gupte — "I'm a Poster Girl for the American Dream," *New York Sun*, January 4, 2006.

Bob Herbert — "The Mobility Myth," *New York Times*, June 6, 2005.

Marcy Kaptur — "Saving Small Farmers," *Nation*, February 6, 2006.

Bruce Katz — "Extending the American Dream," *Boston Globe*, April 13, 1999.

Ellen Florian Kratz and Jia Lynn Yang — "Fear of Falling," *Fortune*, December 26, 2005.

Paul Krugman — "The Death of Horatio Alger," *Nation*, January 5, 2004.

Christina McCarroll — "Suburbia 101," *Christian Science Monitor*, January 11, 2006.

Jim McDermott — "American Dreams," *America*, February 13, 2006.

James Nuechterlein — "American Dreamer," *Commentary*, January 2006.

Joe Saltzman — "No Media Protection Here," *USA Today* magazine, January 2006.

Hilary Shenfeld et al. — "Red, White & Proud," *Newsweek*, July 4, 2005.

Anne Shlay — "Low-Income Homeownership: American Dream or Delusion?" *Urban Studies*, March 2006.

Ilan Stavans   "How Elite Universities Fail Latino
                      Students," *Chronicle of Higher Educa-
                      tion*, January 20, 2006.

Bob Thompson   "No Help Wanted: Author Exposes
                      How the American Dream Turned
                      into a Middle-Class Nightmare,"
                      Washington Post, September 7, 2005.

Mark Trumbull   "Waning Era of the Middle-Class
                      Factory Job," *Christian Science Moni-
                      tor*, December 8, 2005.

Brendan Vaughan   "Who the Hell Is McGraw?" *Esquire*,
                      February 2006.

Fareed Zakaria   "An Immigrant's Faith: The Right to
                      the Pursuit of Happiness Is America's
                      Unique Contribution to Human-
                      kind," *Newsweek*, September 27, 2001.

Internet Sources

Forrest P.   "Adult Literacy and the American
Chisman   Dream," Council for Advancement of
                      Adult Literacy, 2002.
                      www.caalusa.org/
                      caaloccasionalpaper1.pdf.

Gavin Esler   "American Dream Eludes the Poor-
                      est," *BBC News*, September 21, 2005.
                      http://news.bbc.co.uk/go/pr/fr-/2/hi/
                      programmes/newsnight/4265454.stm.

Humphrey Hawksley	"Stark Reality of the American Dream," *BBC News*, August 18, 2005. http://news.bbc.co.uk/go/pr/fr/-/1/hi/ programmes/ from_our_own_correspondent/ 4159974.stm.
Jim Hightower	"Vanquishing the American Dream," *Alternet*, January 24, 2006. www.alternet.org/story/31127.
Andrew Moravcsik	"Dream On America," *Newsweek International*, 2006. www.msnbc.msn.com/id/6857387/ site/newsweek.
Bill Moyers	"The Mugging of the American Dream," *Alternet*, June 6, 2005. www.alternet.org/story/22163.
William Rivers Pitt	"The Other American Dream," *Truthout*, September 1, 2002. www.truthout.org/docs_02/ 09.01A.wrp.am.drm.htm.
Holly Sklar	"The Dying American Dream and the Snake Oil of Scapegoating," *PublicEye.org*, January 3, 2006. www.publiceye.org/eyes/ hs_econo.html.

Index